Cartoon Character
Animation with Maya

Fairchild Books
An imprint of Bloomsbury Publishing Plc
Imprint previously known as AVA Publishing

50 Bedford Square   1385 Broadway
London   New York
WC1B 3DP   NY 10018
UK   USA

www.bloomsbury.com

FAIRCHILD BOOKS, BLOOMSBURY and the Diana logo are
trademarks of Bloomsbury Publishing Plc

British Library Cataloguing-in-Publication Data
A catalogue record for this book is available from the British Library.
ISBN:
PB: 978-1-4725-3367-8
ePDF: 978-1-4725-3382-1
ePub: 978-1-4742-3858-8

Library of Congress Cataloging-in-Publication Data
Osborn, Keith, 1972—
Cartoon character animation with Maya /
Keith Osborn.
pages cm
Includes bibliographical references and index.
ISBN 978-1-4725-3367-8 (alk. paper)—ISBN 978-1-4725-3382-1 (ePDF)
1. Computer animation. 2. Maya (Computer file) 3. Cartoon characters.
I. Title.
TR897.72.M39O83 2015
006.6'96—dc23
2014028447

Typeset by Roger Fawcett-Tang
Printed and bound in China

Cartoon Character Animation with Maya

Mastering the Art of Exaggerated Animation

Keith Osborn

Fairchild Books
An imprint of Bloomsbury Publishing Plc

BLOOMSBURY

LONDON · NEW DELHI · NEW YORK · SYDNEY

CHAPTER FOUR   86
BREAKDOWNS

CHAPTER FIVE   114
REFINE

CHAPTER SIX   138
CARTOONY TECHNIQUES

APPENDIX   170

INTRODUCTION

I'm not going to kid you. Creating cartoony computer animation can be difficult. But as Epicurus reminds us, "The greater the difficulty, the more the glory in surmounting it." Now, that will be the only reference in this book to any Greek philosophy, I promise. I mean, this is a book on cartoons, right? But it does ring true. As with much in life, we place more value on things that are not easily attained. So what are the difficulties in animating in a cartoony style? The way I see it, there are two primary hurdles. The first is the technical nature of implementing these techniques. The ability to bend computer animation to your cartoony will (like having a character smear and distort across the length of the frame) has not been a tool available in most computer animators' toolboxes. Computer animation, as an art form, is still in its infancy, and the tools we're using feel a little crude at times.

The second hurdle deals with the aesthetic considerations of applying these techniques in an appropriate manner. Again, using the same example, knowing when and how much to smear a character is an art unto itself. Much like the budding child artist who discovers that a circle in the upper corner of a page represents the sun, and then the sun tends to show up in that same location in every drawing! Once the ah-ha moment has happened, and the technique is learned, there can be a temptation to use that technique wherever and whenever we can. And, in the case of these traditional animation techniques, discretion is key. Knowing when to use it is just as important as knowing how to use it. My hope with this book is to address both of these challenges. Recent developments in character rigging and tools are making it much easier to implement cartoony techniques in computer animation. Even though the application of these techniques may occasionally try your patience, the end result is often jaw-dropping animation magic.

This book is intended for the animator who is looking to develop a more exaggerated, cartoony, animation style. I try to make the information as easy to digest as possible; nevertheless, this book is not intended for the absolute beginner. That being said, a basic understanding of the animation process and how to animate in Maya is all that is needed to get the most from this text. Since animation is a visual art that involves motion, the book will walk you through the production of a short animated scene, which will incorporate every technique mentioned within. You will have a real-world example from which you can follow and learn. To access this movie file along with the character rig and tools used to create the animation, you can find them at the companion website: **www.bloomsbury .com/Osborn-Cartoon-Animation**. By the end of the book, my hope is that you'll be able to incorporate these techniques into your animation by expanding your knowledge, skills, and toolset.

One more thought . . . As a teacher of animation, I'd be remiss not to speak briefly about learning these techniques and learning animation in general. Early in my career as an animator, I was naive enough to think that you either "had it" or you didn't. Meaning, there were some students who, no matter how hard they tried, were never going to be accomplished animators. I won't deny that learning the art of animation does take longer for some people than it does for those who seem to grasp the concepts early on. Whether that's nature or nurture, I don't know. But what I do know is that eight years of teaching and one person in particular have taught me a very important lesson: dedication matters.

So who is that one person in particular? For the sake of anonymity, I'll call this person "Bryan." Bryan started his animation career as a render wrangler. For those unfamiliar with the job title, this person is responsible for monitoring the farm of computers devoted to rendering out the final images. It's a technical role, one not many artists will find satisfying; nonetheless, it was a foot in the door for Bryan, and one he gladly accepted. Bryan had no real formal training in animation, aside from a class at a local community college. His animation reel consisted of some ball bounce exercises and a weak acting test. But, man, did this guy have passion. He was always asking for input from the other artists and constantly working on his craft. His drive to improve was intense, and he gave it his all. It didn't take long for him to reach his goals. I had the privilege of witnessing Bryan's steady rise up the animation ladder to where, within just a few years, he had become not only an accomplished animator but also an animation lead and eventually an animation supervisor. Fast-forward another handful of years and he's currently the CEO of a boutique animation studio, creating quality work and serving well-known clients. I learned a valuable lesson from Bryan: dedication matters. So expect to be challenged and perhaps even fail at times. I guarantee that if you slog through it, it'll eventually click. In the words of a famous animated fish, "Just keep swimming."

CHAPTER ONE
THINKING IN 2D

When I opened Maya for the first time, I was incredibly anxious. Here I was, an eager art school student, using the same software that many of the big studios were using, getting my first taste of the wondrous world of computer animation. But it was also a very complex and deep piece of software, and it was all very foreign to me. With every mouse click came the fear that I'd break something—and I often did. As computer animation students, we would hear how some of the illustration students were complaining about how complex Photoshop was. Not to diminish their frustrations, but they had no idea how adding that extra D (as in dimension) complicated things exponentially.

As the years passed and I became more and more proficient with Maya, I found myself longing for the simplicity of pencil and paper, to get back to the roots of our craft: traditional animation. My lack of drawing skills meant being a traditional animator was beyond my reach. However, I'd occasionally come across computer animators who were incorporating traditional animation techniques into their workflows. Things like working pose to pose, using stepped tangents, and pressing the comma and period keys to simulate page flipping fascinated me, and I eagerly adopted them into my workflow. As I did this, I found the animation process more challenging but also more rewarding, as I felt more like an artist and less like a technician.

Nowadays, these approaches are more commonplace, and perhaps you already work in that manner. If you haven't explored these approaches, don't worry, we will be covering some of these techniques in more detail soon enough. But before we get into thinking like a 2D animator when it comes to motion, let's take a step back and look at the importance of thinking in 2D with regard to character design and how it will affect your animation.

DESIGN INFORMS MOTION

Unless you're creating the characters yourself, the design of the character is not something you probably have any control over. However, design does have a huge impact on how the character is expected to move, so design is something you'll want to give strong consideration to when thinking about the style of animation you'd like to create.

We expect a certain style of movement based purely on how the character is designed. If a character is realistically designed and rendered, we expect that it will move in a more naturalistic way, carefully following the laws of physics. This expectation can, and often is, played with, as when the Hulk is leaping from building to building in a very nimble way. But there's a point where the believability can be broken.

We don't have to have a PhD in physics to notice when a particular action that a character is performing is not quite right. If the Hulk were to do a broad,

cartoony take with his eyeballs popping out of their sockets, we might be quite amused but we'd also get the feeling that something is off. The Hulk wouldn't look right moving in that manner because he's far too realistically conceived.

Conversely, if an early 20th century, rubber-hose style character, like the original Mickey Mouse, is carefully and precisely following every law of physics, it would look wrong and potentially confuse the audience. Our expectations of movement based on the design of the character may be instinctual, or perhaps they have been groomed by decades of movie watching. Regardless, in general, the more caricatured or cartoony the design, the more freedom you have to explore the style of movement. Even subtle variations make a difference.

Take Genie in *Aladdin* (1992), for example. He has a very curvilinear quality to his design and, appropriately, moves in a very broad and flowing manner. Aladdin, on the other hand,

while caricatured, has some semblance of anatomy, and it would look odd for him to move in the same way. Even in the same film, with a cohesive style, differences in design matter to motion. Thus, a primary consideration when deciding upon the style of movement begins long before animation. Much of it rests in how your character is constructed. If you want more freedom to explore these techniques, it's best to stick with highly caricatured and cartoony characters.

1.1 *Star Wars: The Clone Wars,* **2008**
Clone Wars, with its strong design aesthetic, lends itself to more caricatured and dynamic action.

1.1

DESIGN INFORMS
MOTION

ANIMATING
IN 2D IN 3D

INTERVIEW:
KEN DUNCAN

OVER TO YOU!

1.2

1.2 *The Avengers*, **2012**
Because the Hulk is realistically designed and inhabits a lifelike physical world, he's expected to obey certain laws of physics with which we're all familiar.

Truth in Materials

In computer animation, we have the incredible ability to simulate materials, where the surface of objects can look like their real-world counterparts. This, too, has a significant impact on expectations of movement. If you're animating an object that is made up of hard steel surfaces, like a car or a robot, you'll need to take that into account when animating. Of the 12 principles of animation, as defined by the early Disney animators, the principle that will most likely be impacted by this is squash and stretch. A vehicle with a shiny metallic finish falling from a great height is probably not going to do a rubbery bounce when it lands. That's not to say that you can't use squash and stretch, though. It should be used judiciously and in accordance with what the object is physically made of. A great use of this principle can be seen in the movie *Cars* (2006). Watch this movie with this in mind, and you'll notice the subtle, yet appropriate use of squash and stretch whenever the vehicles move about.

To give another example, I was fortunate to be involved with the computer-animated introduction of the Road Runner and Wile E. Coyote in *Coyote Falls* (2010). Even though the design of the characters closely followed the model sheets from the original traditionally animated short films, the characters were rendered with somewhat realistic feathers and fur.

In terms of animation style, we were able to be snappy and cartoony with the overall timing. However, because Road Runner's tail looked like real feathers, when his body came to an abrupt stop, his feathers needed more time to settle. It was a challenging blend of old and new, and the style of motion needed some exploration before we found something that worked.

TIP

THE 12 PRINCIPLES OF ANIMATION

These 12 principles, as introduced by Disney animators Ollie Johnston and Frank Thomas, in *The Illusion of Life* (1981), are the building blocks of our craft. We'll be going into some of them more deeply and how they relate specifically to cartoony animation throughout the book.

1. **Squash and stretch**

2. **Anticipation**

3. **Staging**

4. **Straight ahead action and pose to pose**

5. **Follow through and overlapping action**

6. **Slow in and slow out**

7. **Arcs**

8. **Secondary action**

9. **Timing**

10. **Exaggeration**

11. **Solid drawing**

12. **Appeal**

ANIMATING
IN 2D IN 3D

INTERVIEW:
KEN DUNCAN

OVER TO YOU!

DESIGN INFORMS
MOTION

Limited Animation

One extreme of the cartoony design spectrum is known as limited animation, where the design is pared down to more abstract, simple shapes. Hanna-Barbera's *The Flintstones* and *The Jetsons* are notable traditionally animated examples. *Pocoyo* (2005) and *Jelly Jamm* (2011) would be more modern computer-animated equivalents.

One of the primary reasons for simplifying the designs is to expedite the animation process, making it less time-consuming, and thereby less expensive to create. Probably the greatest benefit of this strong graphic approach is that you can get away with the character being completely still, moving only what's necessary to communicate the idea. These types of cartoons are often dialogue heavy, so usually the only thing moving on the character is its mouth. In traditional animation, a single drawing can be used for many frames, resulting in considerable cost savings. Likewise, in computer animation, the less a character moves, the quicker an animator can churn out footage. It's a cost-saving approach, as not every animated project can have a Hollywood feature film budget. However, be careful not to correlate limited animation with lower quality.

The animation in *Pocoyo*, for example, is incredibly well-conceived, beautifully executed, and delightfully charming. Watching it can easily bring a smile to your face. Any stylistic extreme, like limited animation, will demand a thoughtful approach to how the

1.3

characters are going to move. Design has a profound impact on motion and when working on a project with a strong design aesthetic, it may not be obvious how the characters are going to move, and some experimentation may be in order.

One of the best ways to experiment with how a character might move is to animate walk cycles. Walk cycles are not always a funfest, but you can use them to roughly block in the primary poses. They can be quickly iterated and used as the testing ground for developing the style of motion for a particular character or even an entire series. Regardless of how you develop that palette of movement, there should be a harmony between how it looks and how it moves—and that may take some tinkering.

1.3 *The Flintstones*, 1960–1966
The animation in *The Flintstones* is a great example of how design can influence the style of motion. The brilliant design of the characters allowed the animators to take shortcuts to stay within a modest budget, while maintaining quality.

Static Holds and Isolated Movement

One of the benefits of caricatured design is that we're able to toy with some of the rules of computer animation, bending them and perhaps even breaking them. Early on in my computer animation career, I was told that I should avoid static holds, where the character is absolutely still, because it looks like the character has gone completely dead. In real life, this is indeed the case. No one is ever completely still (unless they're dead) and because one of the pursuits of computer animation is to mimic reality, we were trained to avoid static holds. However, as mentioned earlier, limited animation employs static holds liberally. Even in feature-quality traditional animation, static holds are used throughout. Background characters are often completely still for seconds at a time. Similarly, main characters will ease into a static hold for a dozen frames. But in the land of computer graphics, this was considered a no-no.

Likewise, I was conditioned to avoid isolated movement, where a part of the character, say an arm, for instance, moved without other parts of the body being affected by it, another no-no. However, in traditional animation, this is a technique that's routinely used, especially in limited animation. And just like static holds, this was a technique that was off limits to the computer animator.

However, films like *Hotel Transylvania* (2012) and *Cloudy with a Chance of Meatballs* (2009) broke from these computer graphics (CG) restrictions and, in the process, created some delightfully amusing moments using static holds and isolated movement. It wasn't that the animators were ignorant of these taboos, unknowingly and mistakenly animating this way—far from it. The graphic stylization of the design afforded them the opportunity to explore these previously closed avenues.

Great care and skill is still needed to know when and how far to push the animation. For instance, a static hold in CG, even with highly caricatured characters, can demand a very controlled ease into that hold in order for it to look right. Even though we're working with visuals that are considerably distanced from realism, the rendered computer-animated image, with its textured surfaces and lifelike shadows, can still make characters appear dead if the static hold is not handled with care. It largely depends on how far a departure the design is from realism. So if your design permits, experiment with new styles of movement, and discover just how far you can push your animation.

1.4 *Cloudy with a Chance of Meatballs***, 2009**
Cloudy with a Chance of Meatballs broke new ground by pushing the boundaries of cartoony action in a computer-animated feature film.

1.4

DESIGN INFORMS
MOTION

ANIMATING
IN 2D IN 3D

INTERVIEW:
KEN DUNCAN

OVER TO YOU!

TIP | ANIMATING WITH A STYLUS

In traditional animation, it makes perfect sense to use a stylus as an input device with a computer. But what advantage is there to using one in Maya? Part of it has to do with feeling like an artist. There's just something about holding a stylus that makes it a more visceral, hands-on experience. More importantly, for myself and many other artists I know, it's a way to help alleviate repetitive strain injury (RSI) that is common when using a mouse for extended periods of time.

If you're thinking of making the transition to a stylus, the best piece of advice I could give is to unplug your mouse as soon as you plug in your tablet. That way you won't be tempted to use it in lieu of the stylus, and you'll dramatically shorten the amount of time it takes to become proficient in its use. In my experience, it took two weeks to get to that point and I couldn't be happier with the results. It's not an ironclad guarantee that you won't experience RSI with a stylus, but it's definitely worth giving it a try if it does indeed help. Just one more tech-tip—I'd strongly suggest getting a stylus with a rocker switch that has two buttons on the barrel. That way you could reprogram one switch to be the middle mouse button and the other switch to be the right mouse button.

ANIMATING IN 2D IN 3D

Aside from character design, thinking in 2D can play a significant role when animating. The great thing is that you don't have to be a master draftsman to think like a 2D animator. We're not talking about developing an entirely new set of skills—we're talking about retraining our brain to look at things a little differently than perhaps we have before. And it's not at all complicated. Next are some simple reminders of things you can do to help you think more in 2D when it comes to animating.

Every Frame Is a Drawing

One of the 12 principles of animation, defined by the early Disney animators, is solid drawing. Although we don't draw our characters in the traditional sense while animating in 3D, I do think it's a good mindset to think of our posed character as a drawing. Why is that? When the final product reaches the audience, it's displayed on a flat screen, so in essence, it's a two-dimensional image, a drawing. But that's more a technical distinction, and I'd like to propose a more artistic one. If we think of our posed character as a drawing, it helps us step out of the virtual world we're working in and examine the image in the more fundamental aspects of good design. By examining our character from the view of a singular camera, we can then evaluate the image from a design standpoint, taking into account things like composition, use of negative space, clarity, straight against curves, contrast, and rhythm.

If some of these terms are foreign to you, don't worry—we'll go into more detail in the following chapters. For now, however, simply remind yourself that the finished product, the final frame, is a two-dimensional drawing. Disney's *Tangled* (2010) is a computer-animated film that exemplifies this idea well. Glen Keane, a Disney traditional animation veteran and an animation supervisor on *Tangled*, used a digital tablet and drew on top of the computer animators' work, showing how the animator could tweak and push the poses to make them more appealing. His great sense of design and his traditional animation mindset shaped the look of the film, and his fingerprints are evident throughout.

Tangled isn't animated in an overtly cartoony style, in the vein of the classic Looney Tunes short films, but the evidence of the 2D-centric approach is clearly seen and felt. It's even truer with cartoony animation, where distortions of a character will look right only if viewed through the main lens. When I really grabbed onto this concept, it became incredibly liberating because I didn't have to fret about what my character looked like from every angle—I was primarily concerned with what was being seen from the main camera. And if it looked right, it was right, even if it was completely wrong from any other point of view. We're playing to the one and only camera that matters, and we can cheat the pose to take full advantage of that. That being said, you may be in a studio or on a production where cameras are seldom locked down, and that approach may not be available to you. This is especially true in video games. With the exception of cinematic cut scenes, locked cameras are pretty rare, and the animation can be viewed from every possible angle. A locked camera is certainly preferred, but even in those instances where it's not available, cartoony animation is not dependent upon that.

DESIGN INFORMS
MOTION

ANIMATING
IN 2D IN 3D

INTERVIEW:
KEN DUNCAN

OVER TO YOU!

1.5

1.5 *Horton Hears a Who*, 2008
Mayor Ned McDodd strikes a pose. Notice the curvilinear quality to the pose, especially his left arm. The standard animation controls of a rig can get the overall pose, but supplemental, secondary controls are necessary to create the curves seen here. It's safe to assume that great care was given to the design of this pose to match the film's whimsical aesthetic.

Abstract Shapes

1.6

One thing that has helped me immensely in doing work that is cartoonier in nature is to think about the character in terms of simple shapes and forms rather than something that is composed of arms, legs, neck, head, and so forth. Why does this matter? Because when you think of things in a more graphic sense, you begin to think about how shapes communicate motion.

A vertical, rectangular shape gives the sense of stability, something that's rigid and still—a lot like a building. However, if that rectangle leans in one direction, motion is implied, as if that object were about to fall over. A stretched triangular shape that's not touching the ground gives the sense of high-speed vertical motion—similar to a rocket lifting off into space.

1.6 *Despicable Me*, 2010
This image from *Despicable Me* illustrates how shapes can have meaning. Gru's top-heavy design, paired with this symmetrical pose with legs tapering into a small footprint, conveys both dominance and instability. The minions are clearly getting on his nerves and he's about to lose his cool.

DESIGN INFORMS
MOTION

ANIMATING
IN 2D IN 3D

INTERVIEW:
KEN DUNCAN

OVER TO YOU!

Shaded View (5 key)   Texture View (6 key)   Silhouette View (7 key)

1.7

1.7 Maya silhouette
You can show your character in silhouette in Maya by hiding any lights in your scene as well as background objects or sets (essentially everything except the character) and pressing the 7 key (display lights). Immediately, you'll see your character in silhouette. Incidentally, pressing the 6 key returns to the texture view or the 5 key for shaded view.

1.8 *Star Trek* teaser poster, 2009
The Starfleet insignia is an example of shape with meaning. The vertical pointer shape gives the impression of an upward trajectory, boldly going where no man has gone before.

One of the easiest ways to mentally shift into this mode is to show the character in silhouette, where the interior details are eliminated and you're just looking at the overall shape of the character, as seen in Figure 1.7. To show you the value of this approach, let's say your character has been shot out of a cannon and is hurtling across the screen at an alarming rate. Designing your pose to look like an elongated arrow, with the arms and legs tucked inside the silhouette of the stretched body, strongly suggests high speed. The more stretched the shape, the higher the implied speed. Contrast that with a strong vertical shape once that character hits a wall, and you've got one heck of an impact.

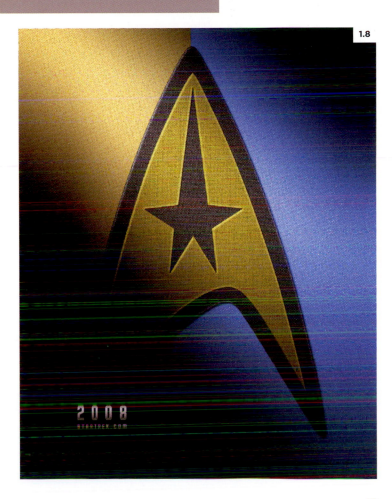

1.8

2008
STARTREK.COM

Every Frame Matters

Like most computer animation software, Maya can interpolate between the keyframes, doing the job normally assigned to an inbetweener if we're thinking in traditional animation terms. However, unlike a skilled inbetweener, Maya doesn't understand arcs and spacing, so it just blindly does the math, filling in the frames between our keyframes. Regardless, the temptation is there to let Maya take care of the frames between our keyframes, as it can be a real time saver. When that happens, where there are long eases in and out of our keyframes, we usually end up with a floaty mess that has no sense of timing.

Just as a traditional animation inbetweener would do, we need to take control of every frame, making sure that there are appropriate arcs, overlapping action, and solid timing in and out of every keyframe. Does that mean we need to animate every frame? Sometimes it does—especially if it's a very fast action that needs to read in a short amount of time. That may sound like an incredibly daunting task, and it is, but it's a mindset that I believe is necessary for cartoony-style animation.

It's important to have control over every frame of the animation. To give you a personal example, on the Looney Tunes CG short film, *Daffy's Rhapsody* (2012), Daffy Duck had to scamper up a ladder before being shot by Elmer Fudd. I only had seven frames to work with to get this done. I pleaded for more frames. But the edit was locked and I had to make do. In this instance, every frame mattered dearly, and I animated every frame, paying careful attention to every part of his body, trying to make it read clearly. After making a few revisions and including a smear-framed foot, I was able to make it happen. Was it tedious? Sure! Was it worth it? Absolutely!

Not only was I able to meet the challenge, but, more importantly, it gave me a newfound appreciation for how precious every single frame is. That 1/24th of a second is the world we live in and during those moments where we're noodling every single frame, trying to get it right, it can be downright frustrating. But I wouldn't have it any other way. Handing the reins over to the world's most ignorant inbetweener too soon is a recipe for a sloppy, gooey mess. So take back those reins and gain some mastery over your motion.

DESIGN INFORMS
MOTION

ANIMATING
IN 2D IN 3D

INTERVIEW:
KEN DUNCAN

OVER TO YOU!

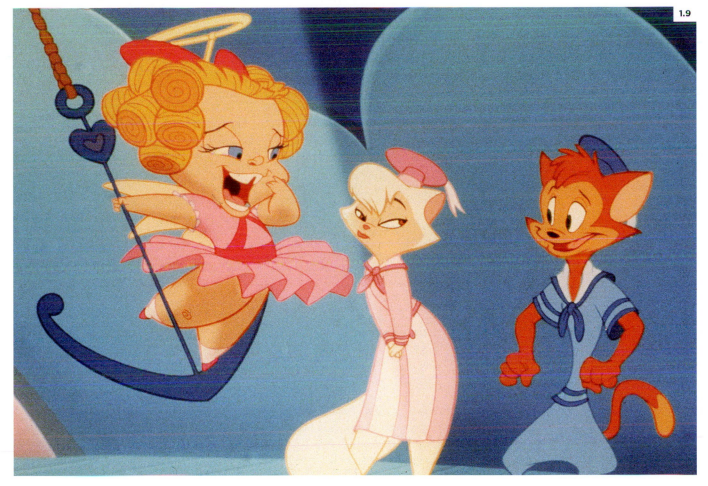

1.9 *Cats Don't Dance*, **1997**
Every frame matters, and this can be seen when studying *Cats Don't Dance* on a frame-by-frame level. Although it didn't break any box office records, it's a beautifully animated film that deserves to be studied and appreciated.

KEN DUNCAN

Ken Duncan is an animation veteran and owner of Duncan Studio. He contributed to many of the classics from the second golden age of animation, including *Beauty and the Beast* (1991), *Aladdin* (1992), and *The Lion King* (1994). In addition, Ken was the supervising animator for Meg on *Hercules* (1997) and Jane on *Tarzan* (1999), and he also successfully transitioned into computer animation, supervising on *Shark Tale* (2004) for DreamWorks Animation.

At Duncan Studio, his company has worked on everything from feature films, to theme park rides, to commercials, to an iPad app. Ken took some time to share his thoughts on transitioning to CG, the future of computer animation, and some helpful advice for animation students.

Can you talk a little about when you made the transition from being a traditional animator to being a computer animator?

The thing about me is that I always wanted to do CG, so it wasn't a transition in a traditional sense, where a 2D guy was being asked to go CG. Going all the way back to when *Tron* (1982) came out, I had seen it and wanted to do CG animation then. I was in an art high school at the time, and Frank and Ollie had just come out with *The Illusion of Life* book about how to do Disney animation. I'm from Ottawa, Canada, and they had the animation festival and they invited Frank and Ollie there to lecture about their new book and they brought in Robert Abel, who had just done *Tron*.

So when I saw the CG stuff and saw Frank and Ollie, I thought, "Wow, it would be cool to mix the knowledge of those older guys with all this new stuff that's happening." I imagined all these great new styles that could be done with computers some day. I wanted to learn CG, and I wanted to learn the character performance style of animation that Frank and Ollie were doing, so that led to me to do 2D at Sheridan College, where I took the first class ever in CG imagery at Sheridan. It was a night class, there were basic vector shapes that you could do; they couldn't even do full CG at the time. It was mostly professional graphic designers from Toronto that were taking the night class, and I think I was one of the few guys in the actual animation program there. So I was always looking out to do CG.

I eventually ended up at Disney, learning the traditional character performance stuff, which, to me, is not really about 2D or CG. Character performance has nothing to do with the tools. It's really about observing people, what's your story, what are the personality types, how do they work into a feature film story, what's the rhythm, what's their posing. And then you can apply it, in my opinion, to either hand-drawn or computer. That, to me, is what you as an animator bring to the table before any machine is involved.

If I were to teach anybody anything, it'd be those traditional principles, you know, what is timing, what is weight, observe reality, what are personalities, what's the psychology of a person, how do they relate to another person, how do they work in the story. I would talk a lot about that stuff before talking about spline curves and stuff like that—not getting hung up on the technology.

Going back to Disney, when things were moving towards CG, I wanted to do more of it, so I started to do a little short film of my own and I was hiring people from the studio to do modeling and rigging, and I was learning more and more on my own.

1.10 *Shark Tale*, 2004
Ken Duncan was new to CG, but that didn't prevent him from putting his 2D animation skills to the test when animating Angie in *Shark Tale*.

It was really in that spirit of trying to continually learn that I was starting to do CG, so there was never sort of a feeling like oh, I gotta learn how to do it because that's where the industry was going. It was always what I wanted to do.

Can you talk about some of the tools and techniques that you used when making the switch to CG?
While I was at Disney, there was a gentleman named Oskar Urretabizkaia who developed tools and ways of working that were very similar to a 2D methodology. Even though it wasn't drawing, it was really about how do you time things and how do you apply spacing to your CG animation. He showed me sort of this methodology and right away I was animating on the side. At that time, DreamWorks was starting to do their first CG film in Glendale, and Janet Healy was a producer who had come from Disney and Industrial Light & Magic and heard that I was doing CG stuff on the side. She just felt there was a value in bringing in people that had experience as character animators as supervisors into the fold onto a CG project. She

interviewed me, and I ended up jumping from Disney and going to DreamWorks, to help put together the character pipeline for *Shark Tale*, and Oskar also went. So we continued to develop some of the tools that he had sort of developed at Disney, at DreamWorks.

So was *Shark Tale* your first foray into computer animation?
Yes. I ended up doing computer animation really for the first time on *Shark Tale*, and I tried really hard to approach it as I would a traditional film. I got into the character—I tried to actually manage one character, which was Angie, the Renée Zellweger character in that film. I would supervise sequences, but mainly sequences with her, and if another character was in the sequence that was not her, I would give it to another guy in my crew, and we would sort of play off each other. He would animate Oscar, the Will Smith character, while I would animate her, and we sort of worked as actors playing off each other rather than doing everything in the shot.

I worked with the timing tools and I worked with an assistant actually, and it was very much the same methodology I had with 2D. So, for example, I would think of posing, much like I would with 2D drawings. I would pose it out, not working on any of the details, try to get the timing

and posing of the personality, show it to the director, get his notes, and then apply the changes. We had an exposure sheet tool, where we could send those poses to that tool and time it out. And that's how I would show my scenes, with my timed-out poses, very much like I would do with drawings—where you scan them, you time them out, you show the director, and then apply notes.

It went really well because I had a methodology already, the way of working and the way I worked with a crew. So with the animators I had under me, I would cast accordingly. If a certain guy was great at action or a guy was good at soft, even spacing, I might give him a certain soft moment with the girl character. And our unit was very fast because we had a system. It wasn't about banging out five versions of a shot, seeing which one sticks. It was really trying to say, okay, this is the reason the character's in the shot, this is the scene in the story, this is how it works, and sort of having a plan before starting to animate. Animators would talk to each other about their characters, and really didn't see it as just one scene, where you move something around on the screen.

It was really about getting into the scene, what was the context, talking to the director, really doing a lot of research before you start animating. It just saves you so much time from

having to do things over and over and over again, trying to guess what people want.

Where would you like to see computer animation go from here?
When I think of 2D, one advantage that it had was that Don Bluth drew a certain way, and Disney folks like Glen Keane drew a certain way. Different people have a certain way of doing things, and it has their imprint. So you have a sensibility of, oh that's that guy's style, that's that guy's film. Warner Bros. had a certain style that was different from Disney, so there was always an attempt almost to have your own look and your own style and to be different.

And sadly with CG, everybody's learning a lot of similar things. They're learning how to animate in a similar fashion, and they're learning how to model things in a similar fashion. Even Tex Avery, his animation style is so different from everybody else, and even in the CG world, you don't often see something pushed that far because that would take an extra effort; the artist would have to know posing and timing a certain way, and there may be films that are close to that, but there's really no demand for it from the studios themselves to push people to do something unique.

It's really about production and getting stuff done because there's so much that rides on a $150 million film, so it's almost going to be smaller independent productions that are going to push the limit. What I love about short films done by students and independents is that they tend to push the limit way more than the studios do because they don't have the limitations to a certain extent and the stress of having to have that box office.

So you feel like CG has stalled stylistically?
I think there's so much more that can be done in CG, I really do. Because of the technology and what you can do with lighting and rendering and things like that, there can be much more of an illustrative style, much more of a surrealistic style, there's much more that can be pushed.

Maybe push your artists to rig in a way that allows for a lot more creativity and freedom, to allow your animators to push things in a different way, and to maybe try to get each animator to have his or her own sort of unique look. That isn't necessarily a negative thing as it is seen in a lot of CG productions now—I see it in a positive way. If a certain animator wants to push a pose in a broad way and another person doesn't, then why not? If that's that person's thing, then maybe find a way of creating some content that actually works to the

advantage of the uniqueness of their ability. It brings a humanness to it, and it isn't just a factory approach to making the films.

If you want to go back to the early days of animation, the 1920s, they were all trying to find a factory approach. That's what happened to animation in those days, whether it was drawing a head using a quarter, or whatever it was, it was just like how can we crank this stuff out, and it all became similar and it all looked the same. In fact, in the early 1920s, animation was really faltering, and even by the late 1920s, it wasn't really a popular art form anymore. Then you had a guy like Disney that said, let's push this art form to another level, and he was constantly doing stuff differently. I'm not saying to copy the Disney approach, or the look, but his sensibility of trying to do something different each time is really the way to look at animation in the future. Really take that concept of how can we do something that hasn't been done. And really try to push the crew to learn new things, in order for them to think of ways of pushing things themselves.

I think there's so much more that can be done in CG, I really do. Because of the technology and what you can do with lighting and rendering and things like that, there can be much more of an illustrative style, much more of a surrealistic style, there's much more that can be pushed.
Ken Duncan

What are your thoughts on animation acting?

When I see some live action films, a character might be doing something in a kitchen, or packing a suitcase, but they're talking about stuff that's much deeper. Maybe it's someone leaving home, and their mother comes in and talks to them as they're packing their suitcase. It has to be something that's in the movie that's like, oh this is a great character moment, but it's not the usual "two characters standing there talking to each other," which to me is getting very boring to watch.

Then you can choreograph the way they are walking around each other in that space, and are they trying to get away from each other, or are they turning away from each other? I don't even hear people talking about this kind of stuff in animation when they're doing sequences. We're not talking about what's the rhythm, what's the subtext, you know, this is the reason why they're turning away.

Even with Oscar, the Will Smith character in *Shark Tale*, I thought he was a character that was so phony to people. He was putting on this act of being this sort of sophisticated confident guy, but he had all these insecurities and he had these dreams of being somebody bigger than he was, and he was kind of a conman. But I always felt when he was talking to people, that he should be trying to evade them so that he would actually turn his head away while he was talking to them, looking around, and not really looking at them eye to eye. So that later, when Angie confronts him on an emotional level, it hits him in the face that he's been a really terrible person. That's when you see his mask fall and he'd be looking at her eye to eye.

So to me, then you have to make that decision early on, like, this is a way to create his performance so that he comes off in a certain way, but it has to be laid out in the beginning. I was just trying to figure out a way to make him a little bit more of an interesting character based on how his personality was, and how you could convey that in his acting. When I'm animating characters, I try to think of people in my own life that I experienced or something I myself have gone through. So if I'm animating Angie, I would actually think of situations where I have been in an argument with somebody, and I could see the reaction of that person when I said something really stupid. Then I would bring those personal experiences to the animation.

What advice do you have for students entering the field?

You always have to think of yourself as an actor or performer, and just forget the computer. Learn it, of course, but use what's going to make you unique, and to me it's all the other knowledge that you might have. Read a lot of stuff, read about the world, read about history, read other types of books, go out and experience what other types of people there are, and just sort of enjoy everything—even the negative things that are in life. They're always going to be there. They're just part of living, and do what you can to draw from all those sorts of things in a positive way, so that when you're animating, maybe you can bring something unique to it.

At Disney back in the day, I had these little lunchtime lectures, and I would show Buster Keaton, Charlie Chaplin, and Harold Lloyd. I personally love silent films, but what I found really interesting about each of those three guys is that they all worked differently from each other, and they were all very successful at what they did. So it's not like one guy was totally copying the other guy. In fact, Harold Lloyd early in his career tried to copy Charlie Chaplin, and it just didn't work at all. So he had to find his own personality, his own character that he believed in to satirize what was going on in life at that time. And so much of animation is like that; it's sort of satirical.

I think in features if you can capture the emotional aspect of it, then that's really the key. It's not just about gags. And basically what we're doing with feature films is we're trying to show people what storytelling really is. We're trying to show people how to deal with problems in life, a guidepost for young people. Like, when you get in a situation, this is how you can overcome it. And that's what any film really is—it's a morality tale, to a certain extent. You may not agree with the villain, but you have to try to understand why he's doing it, and that's really understanding human behavior. And usually it does go back to when they were younger, where somebody made them feel bad, and so they have a need for revenge or whatnot.

Look at what Brad Bird did with *The Incredibles* (2004). The villain was really somebody that was looking for applause. He wanted to be a superhero, not to help people but to get the accolade he feels that he deserves. You know, your villain usually has the same desires as your hero, usually for the wrong reason, and that's where the morality tale comes in. It's like two sides of a tale, and the bad side is the wrong way to live, and the good side is the right way to live, so that's really what we're doing with these films.

But pursuing animation, it's really figuring out why I am doing it. For me personally, it was to tell stories of characters, and how does the character fit into this morality tale, and how can I use my talents to bring my character to fruition? If you're not interested in research, not interested in personalities, and not interested in doing hard work, then I think it's really not the industry for you. A lot of people do get into it because they think it's easy money. If they move things around from a to b, maybe they will have a job for a while, but I don't know how long you'll last in the industry.

I think CG is at a point where the software has become so commonplace that anybody can do it. Some kid in his house can do an animated film, which is amazing. And I said once in a lecture that the Justin Bieber of animation is going to come from that. It's going to be some kid that's really genius at doing character performance and storytelling and he's going to get a couple of his buddies and they're going to make these really inexpensive films that are very popular. So yeah, how do you compete with that? And that to me is to make sure your animation is really strong from a performance standpoint.

In each chapter, I'll conclude with a call to action, something you can do to reinforce the topics discussed within the chapter. This first one is an easy one—watch cartoons. Watch your favorite films through the lens of a designer. It often helps to turn off the audio so that you're forced to look at things purely from a visual standpoint. Look at how the characters are designed and how that affects their movement. Look at shapes and forms that are created and what they convey on a visceral or emotional level.

If it's a computer-animated film, try to forget that it's created in a three-dimensional world and look at it as if it's a drawing or painting, where everything exists on a two-dimensional plane. Also, in looking ahead, I'd like to encourage you to look frame by frame through some of the faster action scenes to see some of the inventive techniques that we'll be covering in Chapter 6. Watch for things like multiple limbs, smear frames, motion lines, and staggers. If you're watching them on your computer, take screen grabs and save them for inspiration and future reference. I'd also encourage you to watch traditionally animated movies, where these techniques are more prevalent. Here are some suggestions of films that liberally use these techniques.

First, I recommend *The Dover Boys of Pimento University* (1942), which is notable for its use of smear frames. Trust me, they are pretty crazy. *Cats Don't Dance* (1997) is a beautifully animated film that has both the Warner Bros.'s snap and Disney's polish and is full of multiple limbs and smears. A third example is *Aladdin*, for the wonderfully fluid Genie animation, again full of multiple limbs and distortions—primarily seen on Genie, but also on Abu. I'd also encourage you to find one of the few examples when Aladdin goes into a crazy distorted smear. Lastly, just about any Looney Tunes or Tex Avery cartoon is going to be jam-packed with cartoony goodness, demonstrating many of these cartoony techniques. By taking the time to watch some of the action frame by frame, you'll be truly amazed and inspired by what you see.

CHAPTER TWO
ANIMATION PLANNING

Starting a new scene can be both an exhilarating and a terrifying experience. Exhilarating in that it's a clean slate, a chance to create something memorable. Plus, we're actually animating for a living—how cool is that? Terrifying in that perhaps this will be the shot that I completely mess up, revealing to the director just how incredibly inept I am. From what I gather, this is a fear shared by many. Planning your shot before you begin, even if it's couch-time, sitting and visualizing the scene, can help prevent the latter from happening. Jumping into Maya right away does, sometimes, work out just fine. There's a chance we'll hit the ball out of the park.

But animators can't consistently operate on chance, expecting to create a great scene every time. Knowing what you're going to do before setting a single keyframe often means the difference between a great scene and just a mediocre one. I've been animating for 10 years now, and I've probably animated about 20 minutes of animation in that time.

However, I'm only really proud of about two of those minutes and of those two minutes, all of them involved some level of planning before jumping into Maya. Planning doesn't guarantee a great scene, but it does significantly increase your chances. The director, and ultimately the audience, deserves the best we can offer, so it's our responsibility to not skip over this step.

At its core, planning is just exploring many different options and choosing the best one. It usually consists of some combination of thumbnail drawings and live-action reference. In this chapter, we'll discuss those planning methods with respect to cartoony animation and how your work can greatly benefit from them. This book is primarily concerned with the mechanics of motion; however, we'll discuss the state of animation acting and how it relates to cartoony animation. Lastly, we'll dive into the planning that went into the animation, *Blind Date*, included in this book, so that you can see the first steps taken to create it.

THUMBNAILS

Thumbnails are simple, exploratory sketches that are wonderful for working out many ideas in a short amount of time. They're an incredibly useful tool for any animated performance. But what distinct advantage, if any, do thumbnails offer when crafting an exaggerated performance? The whole idea of cartoony action is that it's larger than life, an exaggerated interpretation of the natural and real. One of the strengths of thumbnails is that they're inherently a creative endeavor where you engage the right side of your brain to pull from your imagination. This can lead to thinking outside the realm of the natural and give rise to some truly original and entertaining ideas. Because of this, thumbnails are a great go-to when planning a cartoony shot.

Many animators will start with video reference and then do thumbnails based on that. However, starting your planning with thumbnails allows you to approach the scene from a purely imaginative place. Feel free to jump right in and start exploring some ideas. If you're stuck staring at the blank sheet of paper, I would suggest that before you lay down some lead, close your eyes and play the scene out in your mind, visualizing the poses and the movement. And don't judge your ideas at this stage, as you're bound to regurgitate some clichés. It's good to get those out of your head. Simply putting them down on paper can allow you to move past them. Be prolific and fill up an entire page or more with these quick thumbnails. Milt Kahl, one of Disney's animation legends, would create dozens of variations on a single idea, looking for the perfect way to express it. We can do well to imitate one of the great masters of our craft.

2.1 Line of Action
This image of Horton from Blue Sky's *Horton Hears a Who!* is a great example of an exaggerated, cartoony pose. The line of action is clearly seen as it runs through his body and out through his leg, creating a sense of flow within the pose.

2.1

Stick Figures Plus

Keep things simple and don't get caught up in the details. Unless your shot is a close-up and you're working out some facial expressions, I'd suggest not drawing the face at all. The same goes for the fingers. Don't let any perceived inability to draw prevent you from creating thumbnails. I like to think of thumbnails as stick figures plus. And everyone can draw stick figures. Simplicity is key, and you don't need many lines to communicate an idea.

I build most of my thumbnails around the line of action—this imaginary line goes through the character creating a feeling of movement. Unless the character is standing erect, the line of action will usually be a C curve or occasionally an S curve. I then construct the rest of the character around it: a circle for the head, two lines that travel down the sides of the character's body, continuing on down through the legs. Unless both arms are down by their sides or raised up high, I'll sometimes use a single line to represent the entirety of both arms. By paring down the number of strokes you make, not only will you draw faster, but you will also have a sense of flow and connectedness through the character. Also, by working this way, you can avoid a segmented approach to your drawing, and your thumbnails will have a feeling of rhythm and harmony that often translates well when posing your character.

Mission Impossible

Be expressive with your thumbnails. Really exaggerate the poses. See how far you can push the line of action. In addition to pushing the poses, look for opportunities to push the ideas. The only limit is your imagination, so try not to ground it by thumbnailing things that are only physically possible. The sheer size of Tweety Bird's head makes flying a near impossibility. But we don't question it when his tiny wings flap and he takes flight. We also don't question it when Wile E. Coyote can run off the edge of a cliff and be suspended in midair, defying the laws of gravity—that is, until he becomes aware of it. While it's utterly unrealistic, it's completely believable because those are the rules that govern that world.

The closer we move toward exacting reality in cartoon animation, the more we're at risk of jeopardizing believability. With animated filmmaking, we get to play with and bend the rules, which is an awesome privilege and opportunity.

2.2 Thumbnails
In finding the best way to express a character's enthusiasm, I thumbnailed over a dozen variations on the theme, trying to come up with something beyond the obvious, a pose with the arms fully extended in the air. This process takes just a few minutes and can greatly enhance the quality of your work.

VIDEO REFERENCE

Whether it's recording yourself, studying great acting moments from film, or analyzing animal locomotion on a frame-by-frame level, video reference has had a profound impact on animation planning. For many artists, it's become the primary means of visualizing a scene before keying poses. They'll edit the best takes together, and it becomes the foundation for the character's acting choices and for referencing the physicality of the movement. It used to hold the stigma of being a crutch, something that weaker animators relied upon. That stigma has mostly evaporated, and now the animation community largely embraces using video reference as an extremely useful tool. Milt Kahl has an interesting take on it:

> If you use live action for reference, actually, truly just for reference, that's great. I did this with *Jungle Book*. The way to use it, I think, is to learn so much about it that you don't have to use the reference anymore.
> —Milt Kahl, *Disney Family Album*, 1984

So how do we reconcile what an animation legend has to say about using references and how useful it is when working on a style of animation that routinely breaks the rules of physics, something that our gravity-bound bodies can't escape? To answer that question, let's start with how not to use reference, follow that discussion with an exploration of your acting chops, and, finally, consider how to effectively cartoonify your video reference.

How Not to Use Reference

For most character animation and especially broad, cartoony animation, the way not to use video reference is to slavishly copy the physical movement. There's something not quite right when the movement is exactly copied from real life. I believe the main reason is that there's evenness to the timing and spacing of live action that looks off when applied to an animated character. It doesn't stand out so much if the character is realistically proportioned, but it sticks out like a sore thumb when applied to cartoon characters. It seems a bit obvious, but a caricatured character should move in a caricatured way. Achieving realism is not our goal; believability is. It may seem to be a distinction of little difference, but there's a huge gap between the two.

2.3 Animation Planning
Ricardo Jost Resende demonstrates through his planning process how even subtle changes can be meaningful. Notice the slight changes in the thumbnail drawing, based on the video reference, where the pose is pushed to create a more dynamic gesture.

2.3

Can You Act?

When using recordings of ourselves as a means to guide our acting choices, we have to be brutally honest about our acting abilities. Keep in mind that if we're basing the performance entirely on what we're acting out, the animation is only going to be as good as the original material. I've seen some truly expressive, funny, and original acting in video reference. But I've also seen some embarrassingly bad stuff, including pretty much all of the video reference I myself have created.

Part of it simply comes from experience. The more you do it, the more comfortable you'll get in front of the camera. Self-conscious acting is almost always bad acting. But in the grand scheme of things, some of us are just better actors behind a pencil than in front of a camera. Though for those of us who fit into that mold, I still believe there's tremendous value in recording video reference. There can be some truly great surprises that can happen, choices you wouldn't normally invent. Plus it can serve as a springboard to other ideas. You may also have the option of enlisting others to help you out. Whether it's in a studio or in a classroom, there's bound to be someone there who is completely comfortable in front of a camera and is more than willing to assist you. The same holds true for folks you know at home. Surely there's bound to be some goofballs in your list of friends and family.

Cartoonify It

Cartoon characters come with baggage. Certain expectations about their behavior and movement have been cultivated through decades of animation history. That's not to say that we are bound by a certain prescribed palette of movement. There's a diverse and infinite range of motion we can explore. However, we don't want to limit our thinking to just what's observable, as we'd be at risk of ending up with mundane behavior. We want to be careful to not let the video reference take over, dictating every choice.

So how do we avoid this?

I'd recommend scrubbing through the video to look for the storytelling and extreme poses. Take some screen grabs, and then do draw-overs on top of them, finding the essence of the pose and then distilling and exaggerating it to get to the core idea. Once you have those, put the video reference away for now and riff off the draw-overs, creating new thumbnails that are original, fun, and different ways to express the same idea.

Ideally what will happen is that you'll shift gears from being left-brained, analyzing and interpreting the information, to accessing the very right-brained activity of creative exploration. This can lead to some very interesting ideas and can become a solid foundation for when you're ready to jump into Maya.

2.4 Pushing the Pose
Here's another example from Ricardo Jost Resende's planning, this time showing how he went in a more cartoony direction with the pose than what was captured in his video reference. If you'd like to know more about Ricardo's process, check out the interview featured in this chapter.

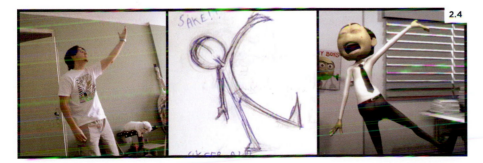

2.4

ANIMATION ACTING

When talking about cartoon animation planning, a lot of time is spent on thinking about the body mechanics and how the character is going to move physically. That's the primary focus of this book. But I'd like to spend a little time on acting and its role in cartoony animation. It's been said that animators are actors with pencils. In this digital age, however, it'd be more appropriate to say actors with mice—though that conjures up a completely different image. Regardless, just because we're working in a style of animation that doesn't necessarily identify itself with Oscar-worthy performances doesn't mean that we shouldn't take acting seriously.

Animation, regardless of the style, is the art of imbuing life into something. To create the illusion of a living being, that being needs to possess the ability to think and feel. That's where the acting comes in and that's how we're going to connect with our audience in a meaningful way. To better understand animation acting, let's consider the style of acting often associated with cartoons, how you might develop and add depth to your characters, and some examples of acting clichés.

Exaggerated Acting

Animation acting is largely stuck in the pre-Brando days. By that I mean the method-acting approach popularized by Marlon Brando, in which acting took a sharp turn toward the natural and nuanced. Prior to his tremendous influence in cinema, acting tended to be more broadly gestured and over the top at times. It was more closely aligned with theater, where the stage actor needs to play to the back row. Even though there certainly are exceptions, animation in general identifies with this style of acting, where we're more likely to see performances akin to Charlie Chaplin than Marlon Brando. And for the most part, audiences are fine with this.

The caricatured design of our characters affords us this freedom, and perhaps even expectation, from our viewers. It's important to point out that broad acting doesn't necessarily mean overacting. When Donald Duck flies into a fit of rage, sure, it's very broad and quite exaggerated, but it's not in any way insincere. He has a volatile personality so it rings true. So we can be truthful and, at the same time, exaggerated. It all stems from who the character is.

2.5 Charlie Chaplin
As an eager animation student, I was turned on to the work of Charlie Chaplin by one of my instructors—and for good reason. His creative, clever ideas and his broad, pantomime acting style are a constant source of inspiration for animators looking to communicate with an audience purely through gesture.

2.6 Marlon Brando
Marlon Brando brought acting to a whole new level of sophistication. Animation seems content to stay more closely aligned with theater acting than the modern method-acting style popularized by Brando.

Creating Character

Most animators put "Character Animator" as their title on their animation reels. But what exactly does that mean? Is it just that we're animating characters instead of props or environments? I think it goes deeper than that. If we're indeed animating characters, then we should be cognizant of the fact that this character is a living, breathing individual with a unique personality and distinct characteristics.

Just as we can identify a close friend far off in the distance, based purely on his or her walk, the characters that we animate should possess individual, identifiable qualities and mannerisms. The physical characteristics of the character will influence how they move (whether they're tall, skinny, short, rotund, etc.), but who the character is has just as much influence. In most productions, who the character is has already been predetermined by the director and/or character lead, and it's your job to make sure your acting choices are true to that character.

In productions where you're in charge, be it a short film you're working on or even an animation assignment at school, you'll likely have greater flexibility, so take full advantage of that and give thoughtful consideration to who the character is during your planning phase. Creating a backstory or history of the character is a good idea. And a great piece of advice is to start with someone you know. It can be a crazy uncle or even a well-known personality. It's okay to steal, but make the character your own and try to avoid stereotypes.

2.7

Johnny Depp, when developing his Captain Jack Sparrow character in *Pirates of the Caribbean* (2003), could have gone with the stereotypical pirate character who grunts "Argh" at every turn, which would have been a shallow and tired characterization. Instead, he patterned his behavior after Keith Richards, the famous Rolling Stones guitarist. In his own words:

> I was reading about the 18th century pirates and thought they were kind of like rock stars. So, when I thought, "Who is the greatest rock 'n' roll star of all time?" It was Keith.
> –*LA Times*, 2003, "Disney loses its innocence with first PG-13 rating."

Johnny Depp came up with a unique take on what a pirate is and created a memorable performance because of it. It's a larger-than-life performance, an exaggerated persona, but it's still truthful. Again, think first about who the character is while planning your shot. The more specific you are, the better off you'll be. This will greatly inform and impact your acting choices.

2.7 *Pirates of the Caribbean, Dead Man's Chest*, 2006
Johnny Depp's performance as Captain Jack Sparrow was largely modeled after the rock-guitar legend, Keith Richards. His acting choices are unique, made manifest by this fun and inspired decision. © 2006 Disney

Animation Clichés

Certain poses have been overdone. But sometimes you may just have to draw from this fount of well-worn gestures in order to get the idea across. I animated one scene where the character was recollecting something from the past. I swore to myself that I was not going to do the Thinker pose. I came up with something else entirely and was really proud that I didn't have to go there. During dailies, however, the supervisor told me that I needed to go with the Thinker pose. I protested at first, but I was reminded that my shot was fairly short and I had to quickly communicate the idea that the character was thinking.

The Thinker pose would fill the bill. Suffice it to say, though, in general, it's a good idea to avoid these poses.

2.8 The Thinker
Popularized by Rodin's bronze sculpture, this pose shows up whenever a character is in deep thought. Add a chin rub and eye darts to go even deeper.

2.9 The Bright Idea
Raised finger + Raised brows = Bright Idea. It's the equivalent of putting a light bulb over a character's head.

2.10 The Finger Point
Closely related to the Bright Idea pose, the Finger Point is extremely useful in situations where you really want the audience to look at something.

2.11 The Fist Pump
The Fist Pump is a self-congratulatory pose that causes the audience to conclude, "I can no longer be your friend."

2.12 The Arm Hold
The Arm Hold is the go-to pose for displaying coyness or insecurity. For female characters, it's almost always accompanied by the equally overused hair-tuck behind the ear gesture.

2.13 The W Pose
Named for the fact that it looks like the letter W, this pose is extremely useful for whenever the character is unsure of something or for when the animator is unsure of what pose to use.

2.14 The Neck Rub
The Neck Rub was brilliant when Baloo from *The Jungle Book* did it. But it's been used so many times since then that it's lost its impact.

2.15 The Hark
"Hark, I hear something." It's the sound of the audience groaning.

2.16 The Three-Point Landing
The Three-Point Landing is seen more often in blockbuster action movies than cartoons. Regardless, it would seem that landing on an even number of limbs is unfashionable.

2.17 Honorable Mention: The Lower Lid Twitch
Since it is isolated to the lower lid, Lower Lid Twitch doesn't qualify as being a pose. Still, whenever a character is stunned or in intense pain, it often makes an appearance so it deserves a mention.

TIP | STUDYING CARTOONS

I've heard it said that we shouldn't study animated films and that we should always go to the source, observing life, or else our work could become a shallow representation of life. While I agree that we should definitely pull from life and life's experiences, I also believe that we should look to the masters of our craft to study how they've approached the challenges we're bound to face.

When learning to draw, it's a common practice to study and copy the masters and through that process learn from them. I believe the same approach should be applied to animation. There's a lot we can learn from studying what they've done. Copying is not the goal and should never be. Learning is the goal. So, cutting off an avenue of learning is something I can't get behind. Notice that we're not watching cartoons to study content, looking for ideas we can lift, and use in our own work, we're watching cartoons to study technique, to see how they dealt with challenging problems. So watch cartoons! Study them frame by frame and discover the inventive solutions that can spur you on to greater work.

RICARDO JOST RESENDE

Ricardo Jost Resende is a recent graduate of Animation Mentor, an online animation school, whose work has been featured in their Animation Showcase. He's a full-time freelance animator who has worked on a number of projects including *The Nut Job* (2014) feature film and the incredibly inventive, interactive short-films *Windy Day and Buggy Night*. He lives in Brazil with his lovely wife and young son. His inspiring animation is the result of his dedication to planning and utilizing video reference, thumbnails, and even some 2D animation. I sat down with Ricardo to find out more about his planning process.

Your animation is often very expressive and caricatured at times. Where does that come from? What inspires you?
Well, I really enjoy when animated films go in a cartoony direction. That reminds me of the old cartoons and some 2D animated television shows. Blue Sky has some great cartoon gimmicks in their movies. *Presto* (2008) is currently one of my favorite shorts with its fast pace and strong poses. *Cloudy with a Chance of Meatballs* has an awesome animation style. It's not a typical squash and stretch cartoon but is stiff with really graphical poses. I also like to follow great animators' reels to see what they are doing, and that inspires me to keep growing.

My preference for caricature performances also comes from live action films. I remember my father buying piles of Charlie Chaplin's DVDs and the whole family watching them and laughing. The silly gags performed by just body language and mechanics makes an entertaining product for the whole family, similar to watching the circus. The human body for this art form is the essential means of expression.

Actors like Chaplin were very expressive and showed very clear attitudes and personalities. Of course, part of this performance was due to the lack of cinematography from that time, but this is the essential key of great animation in my opinion—when the character clearly communicates the idea and entertains the audience without sophisticated cameras and refined dialogue. Even nowadays, we have actors like Jim Carrey who have an impressive visual performance. I remember when I was young watching *The Mask* (1994) and being impressed by the cartoon appeal of that film, partially due to his on-screen performance in this and other films.

Can you describe your planning process?
I try to use every tool at my disposal. I shoot video reference, thumbnail as much as possible, and do 2D animation passes before going into CG blocking. This is a very organic process. Sometimes I shoot video references first, and sometimes I do thumbnails first. It all depends on how the idea for the shot is in my mind. When the footage is too long or if it's more of a pantomime shot, I usually start thumbnailing to figure out the main beats of the story. Even during the CG process, I shoot reference or draw over the Maya playblasts to figure out some specific movements.

When I shoot reference, I try to think like an actor, from the inside to the outside of the character, finding the character's internal motivations.

2.18 Ricardo's Planning Thumbnails

As you can see in Ricardo Jost Resende's thumbnails from an Animation Mentor physicality assignment, only the necessary details are shown. That being said, careful thought is given to the silhouette value of each gesture, so the idea can be quickly read and clearly communicated.

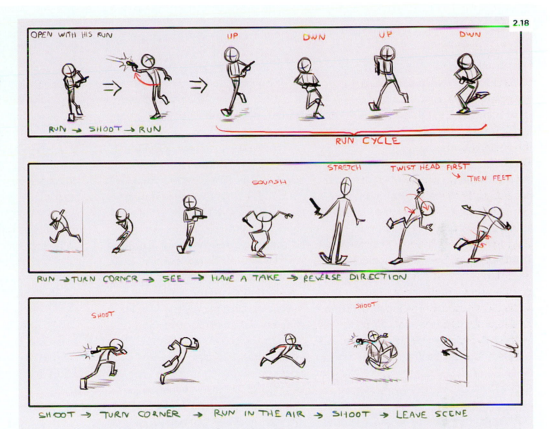

If it's a pantomime shot, I focus on the character's motivations and find some internal dialogue to act it out. If it's a dialogue shot, I like to write down the thoughts behind the phrases. This way, I am doing things instinctively that might help to sell the character and the subtext of the shot. I'm not a good actor, and while I believe an animator doesn't need to be, I do think shooting reference also helps to get some genuine acting choices that can be used in the animation. It's also helpful for caricaturing them later.

After shooting several times, it's time to edit. In this process, I feel like a live-action director choosing the best take for the shot, but with the advantage of mixing more than one take into the same timeline. Sometimes I have more than one option. If so, I strive to get some feedback and then choose the best.

For the thumbnails, I look for good design on the poses that clearly communicates the desired attitude. In this process, I always have a back-and-forth dialogue with myself, such as, "What is this pose telling me?" or

"Is this going to sell the right idea or is it going to be ambiguous?" It's a good time to experiment during the thumbnail process as the sketches usually come quickly. For the first drawings, there is no need for details at all. At this stage, it's more about the gestural, rhythmic, and flow of the body parts. When I feel confident with some poses, I start drawing the contour and reveal the silhouette a little bit more.

Before going to CG, I usually go to Flash and do a 2D animation pass, which is a good way to establish the overall timing of the animation based on the thumbnails and video reference. It's a great opportunity to try different ideas in motion, since I'm already working at the timeline. I keep the drawings very loose at this stage because I just want to feel the animation, not see the animation. I usually emphasize the line of action and the relationship between poses, doing some breakdowns and seeing which parts of the action lines would go where. These decisions can help me see which movements are most appealing. It's important to push the poses and timing here so when I'm in the CG process I can easily dial it back if necessary. The opposite (waiting until in CG process to push timing and poses) is usually harder.

During crunch time, are you still able to thoroughly plan out your shots?
Not completely, but I always try to plan out something before going into CG. I believe the thumbnailing process is the most common tool I use for planning, even if it's just doing some quick sketches on paper. Thumbnailing is a good way to visually get your ideas out there right after receiving a briefing.

For the other stages of planning, it all depends on the style of animation and the pipeline that you're in. For example, if I'm working on a tight schedule and the animation style

must be realistic, just doing video reference might be a good choice for meeting the deadline. However, if I'm on a cartoony project with a tight schedule, exploring the ideas in thumbnails and/or a 2D animation pass would probably be sufficient.

In my short experience in feature length films, I've tried to create a blocking pass as soon as possible so that I can get feedback from the supervisor and director. They just see the Maya playblasts, and nothing before that. So, right after they give me a shot briefing, describing what they have in mind for the shot, I start thumbnailing it, asking myself how I can communicate their ideas with these poses. Sometimes, when the shot needs more acting choices, I shoot some video reference, or when it needs more body mechanics, I do a 2D animation pass. I rarely do both if the deadline is tight.

When using video reference, how do you decide what to push in terms of poses and timing when applying it to your animation?
When you have a good pose on the video reference that you think communicates the right idea, you can push this pose by simplifying the lines. It's like using a gestural approach on figure drawings—you can tell what the character is doing or feeling with just a few action

lines. Having these lines in mind, you can push the pose and exaggerate it based on the line of action and a good sense of design.

As a general rule, the type of line that you put in your pose depends on how the energy is flowing into your character. When the energy is low and the acting must look more casual, the poses are usually made to be more broken, with more S lines, because every movement is overlaid by other movements. But when the energy is high, there is an explosion of emotion, so the line of action is less broken and tends to be in a single arc. When a force is building from some part of the body, you'll probably have a sharp angle in there. At the end, you have to discover a good balance between these concepts, thinking about where the force is coming from and where it's going.

To push the timing from the reference, I look for times when the movement speeds up and when it holds. A good piece of advice is to explore speeding up or slowing down the footage in the editing software. Generally, fast motion works best for the cartoony effect, and it looks funnier. If you see the old black-and-white movies, you'll see that these films used to play in a faster motion than real time.

What challenges do you face when translating your ideas into CG?

The first challenge is to transfer the lines of action from thumbnails into CG poses, and making them as flowing as possible, as well as working on the silhouette. If the rig doesn't have bend controls for arms and legs, it's not a problem at all. The key is the position and rotation of the joints so they form a fluid line. It's a challenge, too, figuring out the twists of the torso, as the thumbnails usually don't have this information. The twists can make your pose dynamic and also help to show the physicality of the character.

I also like to consider the deformation of the mesh. If this is for a feature film, the mesh usually has textures and lighting applied, so it's important to see how your character is deforming in a CG space. Especially when I'm animating fat characters, I've learned that it's not about line actions and twists, as they usually are not so flexible, but it's more about squash and stretch and the overall silhouette of the pose.

What advice do you have for students looking to push their work into a more cartoony direction?

Keep in mind that every pose expresses attitude, be audacious, make it huge, and you will sell it to the audience. To find those poses, shoot references and make the acting genuine. Translate it to paper, finding the action lines, making it graphical. Do a pencil test and explore more opportunities, feel the movement, and be loose on the sketches.

Never forget the physicality. Use the rules to your advantage but, at the same time, have the freedom to break the rules. It's great when the audience sees something that is impossible to do but feels right. Learn from the old films, where the actors use their physicality to their advantage to make the performance great and entertaining. Having a touch of reality in cartoons makes it more believable.

And have fun!

Learn from the old films, where the actors use their physicality to their advantage to make the performance great and entertaining. Having a touch of reality in cartoons makes it more believable.
Ricardo Jost Resende

STEP-BY-STEP WALKTHROUGH

In providing animated examples for this book, I decided to create something that included all the techniques presented. Instead of doing a series of different animations with each focusing on a separate technique, I created a single animation that would demonstrate them all. You can view and download the film and rig at the companion website.

Here's the concept behind the animation: Mr. Buttons, a happy-go-lucky cat, is on his first blind date. He confidently approaches his date's house and knocks on the door. When it opens, his not-so-subtle reaction reveals his surprise.

In planning for the animation, because I was going to incorporate broad cartoony-animation techniques, I decided to stick with thumbnails. Because most of the actions are highly physical and, frankly, impossible to do in live action, shooting video reference probably wouldn't have been of much use and would likely result in injury to myself. What follows are my exploratory ideas, including the discarded ones. I've circled the poses that I liked, forming the foundation of my performance.

I'd like to point out that even the best-laid plans of mice and men go astray, and there will be changes throughout the animation process. Most of the changes come about during critiques. Either you, your peers, your supervisor, or the director will find a better way to communicate the idea. Some of these changes can be very time consuming to implement—especially if they come late in the game. But this is normal. It's a very fluid process, so expect these changes and have the mindset that it's the best idea that wins.

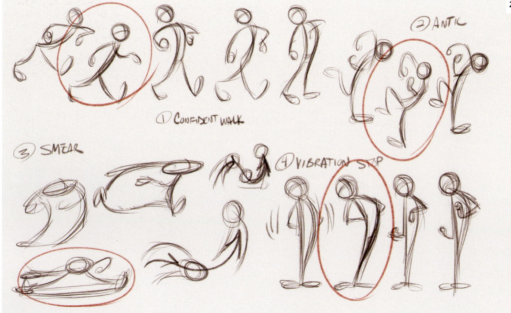

2.19

2.19 Mr. Buttons approaching
This page of thumbnails is all about Mr. Buttons's approach to the house. Instead of having him just walk up to the door, I thought I'd have a little fun by having him walk a few steps, pause, anticipate, and then smear into a stop.

2.20 Mr. Buttons grooming
Here Mr. Buttons, in addition to knocking and presenting flowers, is licking his paw and slicking back his hair. I thought it would be a fun bit of business—something a cat would do.

2.20

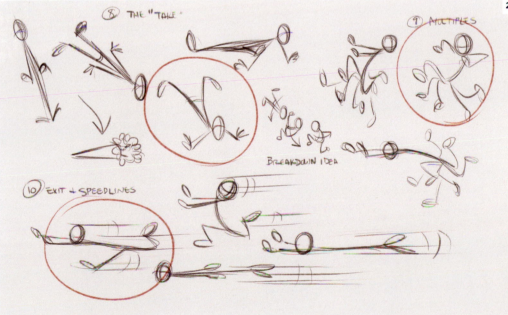

2.21

2.21 Hightailing it outta there
Finally, we have his Tex Avery-style take, which I planned on staggering into. I also decided to use multiple limbs for the scramble and incorporate motion lines when he exits quickly.

OVER TO YOU!

Mr. Buttons is ready and waiting for you to bring him to life! However, as this chapter has demonstrated, animation begins before you even set your first key in Maya. It begins in the planning stage, where you generate your ideas and think through all the choices beforehand. I'd like to encourage you to follow along with me and animate your own shot. You can do something similar or something completely new.

Perhaps Mr. Buttons could be enamored with what he sees when the door opens. Or he could be the timid type, knocking on the door and quickly ducking behind the house, head peeking out to see who opens the door. Or Mr. Buttons could be doing something entirely different—it's completely up to you. Whatever you do, try to think BIG! Not BIG in terms of length, as you'll want to keep it short, but BIG in terms of style and story. Exaggeration, one of the key principles of animation, is what sets it apart from live action, so we should capitalize on it, bringing a sense of the extraordinary to our craft.

Your planning doesn't have to be exhaustive. It can take as little as a half hour to quickly shoot some video reference and or thumbnail out some sketches. Regardless, it's time well spent. Whether you utilize video reference, thumbnails, a combination of the two, or something else entirely, simply taking some time to think through your shot will likely save time in the end and increase the probability that you'll create animation that's both memorable and something to be proud of. Take that time now and have fun coming up with some wonderfully wacky ideas as I guide you through each step in this process.

After you've planned out your shot, we'll begin posing Mr. Buttons in Maya in the next chapter!

CHAPTER THREE
THE POSE TEST

You're ready to animate! You've got your plan in hand, and you're anxious to start setting keys and breathing life into your virtual puppet. This chapter will focus on the first animation pass, the pose test.

What exactly is a pose test? Put simply, it's a test to see if your poses are reading, communicating what you're hoping to convey to an audience. It's the foundational, storytelling poses—the bare minimum needed to get your idea across. For most shots, it's typically just a handful of poses. With a pose test, you're generally not concerned with things like lip-sync, hair, or clothing. Sometimes you're not even posing the hand, though I'm no fan of the default, Ping-Pong

paddle hand—more on that later. You want to iterate quickly, so you're not getting caught up in unnecessary details. This approach will allow you to make broad changes to your work based on feedback. This pass is also often referred to as blocking—same thing, different term. I like to use the term pose test because it's more descriptive and harkens back to the old 2D days.

Whatever you choose to call it, it's probably the most enjoyable part of the process, as you're beginning to see your character come to life. In this chapter, we will go over some important things to keep in mind as you're starting your shot, especially as it concerns cartoony-style animation.

SCENE PREP

Before we set our first keyframe, we first need to prep our file and think about our workflow. So, let's take some steps now to ensure we're starting off on the right foot.

We'll start with referencing. What does referencing your assets have to do with cartoony animation? Absolutely nothing. However, it's an industry practice, and if you're not already doing this, you should. Referencing is when you bring the character into your scene without that character actually residing in that file. Instead of opening up a character file and beginning animation on that file, you start with a new file and reference in the character, maintaining a separation between the two files while still being able to work with the character. Any changes to the character file will be automatically updated in your animation file every

time you open it. One of the benefits of doing this is that it adds a layer of protection—meaning, you won't be able to accidentally delete a part of the rig when working in your animation file. Second, it keeps your file size small, as the only data stored in your file is the animation data, not the character rig. Because the file size is small, you can

easily save many iterations of your file while you're working, without it taking up a lot of space on your hard drive. I highly recommend that you save many iterations, as I've seen student files get corrupted more times that I can count! So how does one reference in a character rig? Simple: go to File > Create Reference. The defaults are fine.

3.1 Referencing
In every studio I've worked for, referencing is how assets are brought into a scene. Even cameras can be referenced to prevent the accidental deletion of the camera or the editing of its animation. When working on your own, be sure to adopt this practice as a part of your scene prep.

SCENE PREP

DESIGNING
THE POSE

A PRINCIPLED
ANIMATION

INTERVIEW:
MATT WILLIAMES

STEP-BY-STEP
WALKTHROUGH

OVER TO YOU!

Lock Your Camera

I touched on this in the first chapter, but it's worth expanding upon. When tumbling around the character in a computer-animated scene, it's easy to think of your characters and the world they inhabit in the third dimension. With the recent theatrical push to produce films in 3D, it further reinforces this idea. When doing more broad, cartoony-style work, it's critical to divorce yourself from this notion. The rendered image is a two-dimensional plane. It's akin to a drawing on a piece of paper (incidentally, the roots of our craft). There's nothing 3D about it. Even when working on a stereoscopic production, where you have a left and right "eye" creating the illusion of three dimensions, you're still essentially working with a flat canvas, as the slight differences between the two images are negligible.

In order to take full advantage of this concept of thinking in 2D, you need to lock down your renderable camera. In a production, this is already done for you. It's a pretty rare thing to receive your shot from the layout department with an editable camera. When working on your own, it should be one of the first things you do when starting your shot. Before keying a single pose, adjust the camera to effectively stage the character within the environment. Then, once you have a pleasing composition, lock your camera.

As a teacher of many students, I've seen it time and time again, where the student is animating in 3D as if a camera didn't exist. This may be appropriate in certain contexts, such as video game animation, but if the end output is film, you're doing yourself a disservice by working in this way. Although it may seem liberating, it can actually have the opposite effect, hampering your thinking and limiting your ability to come up with creative solutions. Locking your camera will help you to think in 2D. Granted, you'll still need to tumble around the character in order to have access to all the controls and to fully manipulate the rig, so it's a good idea to create a workflow where the renderable camera and perspective camera are visible at the same time. I can't think of a simpler and more practical way to help your brain shift to a new way of thinking than to perform this task. Locking the camera couldn't be easier; just drag-select the camera channels in the channel box, right-click, and choose Lock Selected from the pop-up menu.

3.2 Lock selected
Locking your camera is quick and painless. As you animate, you may find that the camera needs to be adjusted slightly for better staging. However, that's not justification to keep it permanently unlocked. In those cases, simply unlock it, change it, and lock it again.

Breaking the Rig

Because we're only concerned with what's being displayed through a single lens, it gives us the freedom to break the rig and create some truly fantastic images. Now I'm not talking about literally breaking the rig to where it's no longer usable (though that can happen). I'm talking about doing whatever is necessary to achieve the desired results.

Extreme deformation, geometry penetration, off-balance poses, and broken joints are often the norm. To give you a personal example, on *Daffy's Rhapsody* (2012) I was animating a shot with Daffy Duck descending from above, towards the camera, on a rope, twirling around in a very elegant, Esther Williams-like manner. However, in any view other than the renderable camera, Daffy was anything but elegant. In order to create a greater sense of depth, as Daffy was descending, feet first, toward the camera, I had to scale Daffy's feet to over twice their normal size so they appeared much larger in the frame than the rest of his body. To further push the 3D effect, Daffy's torso was elongated to over five times its length to make Daffy's head and upper body appear smaller in the frame. It looked completely fine in the camera, but we were cheating big-time, and any other view would show just how completely broken Daffy was. The illusion only worked through that one camera and by breaking the rig.

3.3

We need the freedom to do whatever is necessary to the rig to create the pose we're looking for. As long as it looks right through the renderable camera, it is right! Working like this may cause some level of anxiety in some artists, but you must be absolutely brutal to your characters, being willing to subject them to any and all forms of distortion and duress. Don't worry, though. They'll rebound in the end. They always do.

3.3 Broken rig
When looking through the perspective camera, Mr. Buttons is clearly broken. However, he is broken for a reason—to get the exaggerated pose that's seen through the renderable camera. Be willing to do what it takes to get the pose you want.

DESIGNING
THE POSE

A PRINCIPLED
ANIMATION

INTERVIEW:
MATT WILLIAMES

STEP-BY-STEP
WALKTHROUGH

OVER TO YOU!

SCENE PREP

Workflows

Which workflow you use is largely a personal choice. However, there are some distinct advantages certain workflows can provide, especially when dealing with cartoony animation. And speaking of workflow, the Disney veterans even dedicated one of the 12 principles of animation to it. Number seven on the list is Straight Ahead Action and Pose-to-Pose, which describes two different approaches to drawing an animated scene.

With Straight-Ahead Action, as the name implies, you simply start from the beginning and animate from that point on, moving forward in a sequential, straight-ahead fashion. With Pose-to-Pose, you're not limited to working sequentially. You could start with the first pose, the last pose, or somewhere in between. Once you've established those poses, you can then fill in the gaps, creating breakdown drawings between the actions and then the in-betweens, filling in all the missing drawings to create fluid and cohesive motion.

With computer animation, those two approaches are still used, but because of the greater flexibility the software provides, we can mix and match and discover ways of working that better suit our own personal preference or are better suited to the style of animation we're trying to achieve. Here are three common workflows in computer animation and how they relate to cartoony animation.

Layered

Layered animation has its roots in the Straight-Ahead Action approach in that you start from the beginning of the scene and move forward sequentially. The primary difference, however, is that you're not animating the whole character at the same time. For most movement, you'd start with the root of the character, the main control that drives the body, and animate that independently, creating the base motion for which to build upon. In the case of a walk cycle, for example, you'd start by moving the root of the character forward, focusing on a single axis of translation (usually the z-axis) until the character leaves the screen or comes to a stop. It's also important to note that the tangent type commonly used with this approach is spline. This allows you to scrub through the timeline and see the movement at every frame.

After you've established the character's forward momentum, you'd then animate the up-and-down movement, getting the bounce of the walk just right. You'd continue to build the walk cycle, working outward from the root of the character, moving up the spine, out through the arms and so forth, layering the motion as you go. One of the benefits of working in this way is that it's mechanically sound—meaning, most action originates from the hips, so the physics of the animation feels right. It also tends to create beautiful, fluid motion that doesn't have the pose-to-pose feel, a common criticism of that approach. Layering was largely used at Pixar in the early days, so it's a very old-school computer animation approach.

**3.4 Graph Editor:
the layered approach**
The layered approach, while producing an anxiety-inducing mess in the graph editor, is a very methodical and logical approach to animating and is especially useful for creating overlapping action on those "floppy bits."

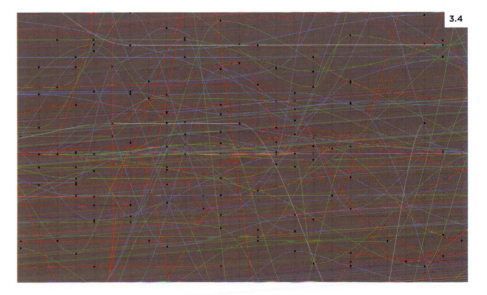

3.4

When Brad Bird joined Pixar to helm *The Incredibles* (2004), with his traditional animation background, there was a push to use a more pose-based workflow, but there are plenty of animators who still worked with a layered workflow at Pixar and elsewhere. It was the de facto standard for animating when I first started my training at the turn of this century. One of the cons of working in this way is that it's difficult for some directors to know how the shot is going to look until it's largely finished. It's difficult to critique something if all you see is a character, in the T-pose, sliding across the screen. It's also an approach that sometimes makes changes difficult to implement, since there are no clear poses that can provide a way of sectioning off what can stay and what can go.

Layering is not as commonly used today, as most computer animators have adopted a pose-to-pose workflow. In terms of its use in cartoonier-style animation, it's even less prevalent because so much of cartoony animation is based on strong poses. It just makes sense to use a workflow that's pose-based. That being said, I still use the layered approach when appropriate. One scene I worked on in the Looney Tunes short film, *Rabid Rider* (2010), had Wile E. Coyote riding on a Segway, being dragged behind a Lamborghini after he had lassoed it with a rope. Since his movement was dependent upon the movement of the Segway, I animated the Segway first, layering in the translation, and then moved to the rotation of the vehicle. I then shifted to Wile E.'s movement, layering his animation from his hips outward. There was also a trailing piece of rope that I animated, layered-style.

Layering is great for "floppy bits," things like rope, hair, ears, tails, and clothing, where the overlapping action of those objects are better realized when layered on top of the main action. In those cases, I'll save those parts for last, after the primary character animation has been completed. I'll also start from the base of the object and work sequentially toward the last control in the chain. For example, if I'm animating a tail, I'd start at the base of the tail, paying close attention to the movement of the hips, making sure the action is dragging behind, and then move on to the next joint in the chain, working toward the tip. It's the kind of work that I consider icing on the cake, as most of the tough stuff has already been handled and I can relax, put on some music, and enjoy the process. While the layered workflow may not seem immediately useful for cartoony animation, it's worth experimenting with and can be, at times, the perfect go-to when warranted—especially for those floppy bits.

SCENE PREP

DESIGNING
THE POSE

A PRINCIPLED
ANIMATION

INTERVIEW:
MATT WILLIAMES

STEP-BY-STEP
WALKTHROUGH

OVER TO YOU!

Copied Pairs

This technique has its feet firmly planted in the pose-to-pose approach to animating. The primary distinction is that you're duplicating each pose, to hold that pose for a number of frames until the next transition, thus the term *copied pairs*. If you're working with stepped tangents, this approach may make little sense because the nature of stepped tangents is that nothing is moving until the next keyframe. So most animators who work in copied pairs use plateau tangents. Plateau tangents eliminate the overshoot seen with spline tangents, creating a truly held pose when creating copied pairs. It's a great method for getting the timing of your work nailed down early on because you get to see how long the pose is going to be held for as well as how quick the transitions are between each pose.

There are two big pitfalls to avoid when working in this way, however. The first is that it inherently creates a pose-to-pose look, which can make the animation appear stilted. Once you hit a pose, it's completely still unless you work to avoid that. You'll need to make sure you're easing into the hold and adding overlap to your actions to make it look more natural. A saving grace is that cartoony animation tends to be very posey anyway, so there's a fair amount of forgiveness here. The other pitfall is that when working with any tangent type that interpolates between your keys

(essentially anything other than stepped tangents), there's a tendency to not give much thought to creating effective breakdowns, since the character is already moving between the poses.

We'll talk about breakdowns in Chapter 4, but breakdowns do two key things—define arcs and determine what leads and follows. Maya stinks at both of these. That's your job, not Maya's, and if you're watching Maya's interpolation between the poses as you repeatedly play the animation, the more you see it, the less objective you become and may simply accept it as being "good enough." If you haven't tried copied pairs, give it a go, but be mindful of these pitfalls. It's a great and effective approach when creating cartoony animation.

3.5 Graph Editor: copied pairs
Copied pairs creates a clean and tidy graph editor, making editing it later on a relatively easy task. This is especially true if you need to retime your animation, as you can clearly see the holds and transitions.

3.5

Stepped Tangents

Stepped tangents is not exactly the ideal name for this workflow—it is, after all, just describing the tangent type used for animation curves—but it is the one, unique tangent type that doesn't interpolate between the keyframes. This workflow is the computer animation equivalent of pose-to-pose traditional animation, where you create a pose, create the next pose, add some breakdowns in between, and then proceed to fill in the remaining gaps with Maya's help.

This approach is the most popular workflow, especially as it relates to cartoony animation. Why is that? Probably because it has its roots in 2D, as stepped tangents create the illusion that you're creating individual drawings that don't change until the next drawing. It's also perfect for control freaks, like me, who don't want to hand over the reins to Maya too soon. It's also a very clean way of working, in that, typically, every part of the character is keyed whether it's moving or not, which creates a very clean and easily editable foundation. Plus, there are no offset keys to muddy up the graph editor.

So what's the catch? It sounds like it's all rainbows and butterflies, and, for the most part, it is! Granted, I'm revealing my bias here, but I do believe it's the best approach to animation when working in a cartoony, broad style. However, when working in a stepped style, there's a natural tendency to want to jump ahead and spline the curves too soon, the end result being a soupy mess, where the animation smoothly eases in and out of every pose. Since stepped tangents naturally produce a hold, as soon as you switch tangent types, your holds are gone. The key is to plan for that and create copied pairs, or a slow-in pose before the final pose—we'll get more into that later on as we cover breakdowns. You have to resist the urge to spline the curves too soon. Take control and make sure you're setting enough keys to prevent soupiness.

You don't just want to set keys willy-nilly, though. Every key should be purposeful. Either a storytelling pose, an extreme action, or a breakdown reveals the arcs and overlap through the transition. Care should be given to every keyframe you create, making sure it's necessary and well thought out. The goal of stepped tangents is to take as much control over our work as possible so that it's not left up to Maya to do its thing.

Even though I am advocating the use of stepped tangents, and the animated example in this book follows this workflow, that doesn't necessarily mean you should wholeheartedly embrace it yourself. The beauty of Maya is that there's a myriad of ways to get the desired result. You've heard it said that it's the journey that matters, not the destination. However, in animation, it's all about the destination. How you get there is irrelevant; all that matters is the result on screen. By all means, explore different ways of working. Chances are that your own personal workflow will evolve as you progress as an animator, but you should ultimately stick with what works for you.

SCENE PREP

DESIGNING
THE POSE

A PRINCIPLED
ANIMATION

INTERVIEW:
MATT WILLIAMES

STEP-BY-STEP
WALKTHROUGH

OVER TO YOU!

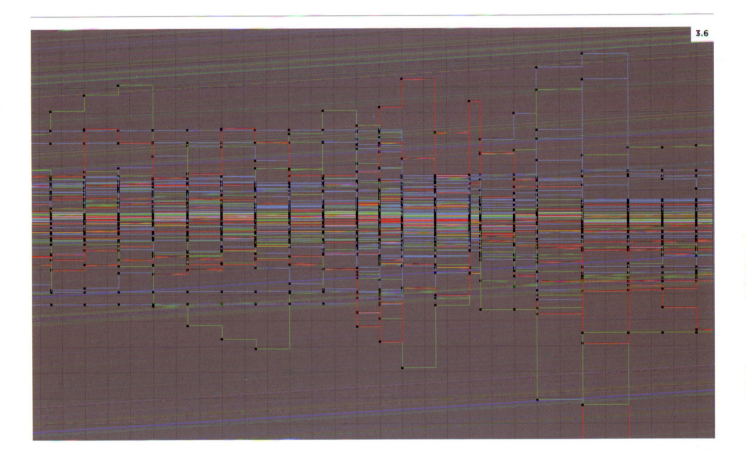

3.6

3.6 Graph Editor: stepped tangents
Stepped tangents are a thing of beauty. They
look like a stairway to heaven in the graph editor.
Unfortunately, unless you plan on keying every
frame, those steps will eventually have to be
turned into slopes. But if you have enough keys
and breakdowns, you can minimize the pain when
making that transition.

A Word on Gimbal Lock

Even though this book stresses the importance of thinking like a 2D animator and adopting practices that simulate a 2D workflow, we can't ignore the fact that we're working in a three-dimensional, mathematical environment. Sometimes that math can get us into trouble, and the prime example of this is gimbal lock. Without getting too technical, gimbal lock happens when the rotational axes of a controller align and "lock," preventing full and free rotation. We'll talk about ways to address and fix this when discussing the different parts of the animation process in this chapter and the ones that follow. But for now, it's important to point out that whichever workflow you choose, be careful when rotating parts of the character—especially those parts that usually have a high degree of rotation, such as the main body control, head, arms, wrists, and ankles. If you want to try to prevent it from the get-go, double-click on the rotate tool and choose Gimbal from the tool settings. This shows you exactly what each rotational channel is doing and can go a long way toward reducing gimbal lock in your animation.

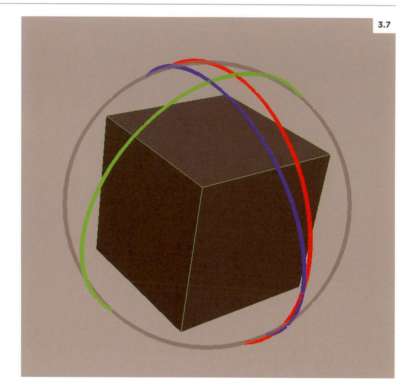

3.7

3.7 Gimbal mode
I'm a huge fan of using local rotations because it's just easier to pose things out that way. But it's also the leading cause of gimbal lock. This image illustrates how we can use Gimbal mode to see when gimbal lock is happening. The X rotational axis and the Z rotational axis are almost in alignment, which can cause problems down the line when we spline our tangents.

SCENE PREP

DESIGNING
THE POSE

A PRINCIPLED
ANIMATION

INTERVIEW:
MATT WILLIAMES

STEP-BY-STEP
WALKTHROUGH

OVER TO YOU!

TIP | CREATE A SELECT-ALL BUTTON

This is pretty basic stuff, but I was always surprised to see advanced computer animation students working without a select-all button for their character. When working pose to pose with stepped tangents, it's important to make sure that for every pose you create, you're keying everything on the character. First, it keeps things nice and tidy in the Graph Editor. More importantly, it ensures that every part of the character is locked down so that when you go spline, there aren't parts of the character swimming around, with a mind of their own because they weren't keyed.

Some animation rigs come with a graphical user interface (GUI) that often includes a button for selecting every control on the character—which is great. But for those rigs that don't, it's good practice to create your own. So how do you do this? Start by opening up the Script Editor by going to Window > General Editors > Script Editor, or you can click on the Script Editor icon in the lower right corner of Maya. With the Script Editor open, select all the controls of the character and look for a line to appear in the Script Editor's history (upper panel) that starts with "select." Select this line of text and left-mouse-button drag it to a place in your shelf. If prompted with the script type, choose MEL. Just be careful that you're selecting only the character controls and not joints or the character geometry, as that can inadvertently break the rig when keyed.

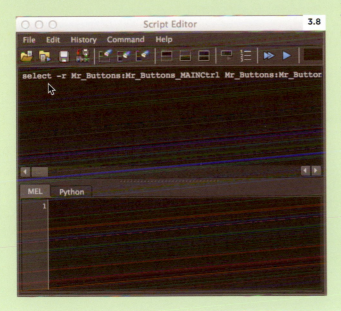

3.8 Select all
Here's the output from Maya's Script Editor when I select all the controls of the character. To make a button from this, select the text, and then left-mouse-button drag it to your shelf.

DESIGNING THE POSE

Poses are the foundation of animated storytelling. Even though much of the focus in animation is on motion and creating movement that's appealing and believable, it's the pose, those brief moments of quiet, where the story is told. As Ham Luske, director of many classic Disney films, has said:

> Your animation is only as good as your poses. You can have good timing, good overlapping action, and good follow through—but if your poses are not strong and to the point (telling the story) you do not have good animation.
> —Quoted in Eric Larson, *Pose-to-Pose and Straight-Ahead Animation*, 1983

Since a pose is a visual representation of an idea or feeling, it should be designed in a way to support that idea or feeling. I know that may sound a bit esoteric, but there are some practical things you can do, some techniques you can apply, that will help you create poses that are both appealing and communicative.

Silhouette

As we touched on in Chapter 1, if there are no lights in your scene, you can put your character in silhouette by pressing the 7 key. Again, you may have to hide the set to see this. It completely reduces your pose to a graphic shape. This is a very useful cheat because it allows you to see if the pose will read at a distance or a quick glance. Many times, a pose will only be held for a fraction of a second, so it's important to make sure that what you're trying to say comes through clearly. One caveat is that there's a tendency when using this technique to jump to the conclusion that it's all about making the pose larger than life, to exaggerate to the extreme, so that every limb of the character is out in open space. Striving for clarity is indeed the goal, but it shouldn't be sacrificed at the expense of sincerity.

To give you an example of how you can apply working in silhouette but still maintain a truthful moment, let's say we're observing a character from across the street. He is walking along the sidewalk and tips his hat to an attractive passerby who walks between the character and the viewer. When he tips his hat, if you use the arm that's closest to the camera, chances are that arm is not only going to be crossing his face (from the camera's point of view), it's also going to be largely lost in the silhouette. By using his other arm it'd be much easier to stage the pose so that the arm is out in silhouette. Notice that we're not changing the amount of exaggeration in the pose, making it grander than it needs to be, we're simply staging it in a way that offers a better silhouette for the sake of clarity.

One exercise I gave my students was to create a short animation, entirely in silhouette, to see if it would read. Plus, they couldn't use any audio or dialogue to help sell their idea. It really cemented the importance of silhouette. It's a fun challenge, but the use of silhouette shouldn't just be relegated to an experimental assignment. Regularly check your poses in silhouette to see if they're reading and if there's a better way to pose the character.

3.9

3.9 *Rio*, 2011
Rafael the toucan with his wings extended into open space is perfectly silhouetted, showing his openness and gregarious personality. Even though Blu's wings are tucked in, his profile in silhouette reveals not only a strong graphic representation of a parrot-like form, but also, with his head pulled back, shows his nervousness—a personality trait we see throughout the film.

Straight against Curve

3.10

Straight against curve is a design principle that incorporates contrast by avoiding perfect symmetry in the parts of the body. Take an arm, for instance. If each section of the arm is curved outward, it's going to look like linked sausages and not be very appealing. Likewise, having each section perfectly straight creates a mechanical and stiff look. By having one side of the arm straight and the other side curved, there's a nice contrast and it creates a much more appealing shape.

Applying a combination of straights against curves throughout the pose creates a beautiful balance. Practically speaking, how does one achieve this? Granted, much of this depends upon the design of the character and the flexibility of the rig. For example, we can get some mileage out of the use of bendy controls. Most modern rigs include controls in the middle section of an arm or leg segment that give the animator control over the shape of that area, allowing you to bend or bow that section. Adding the slightest bend to the arm or leg can create a straight against a curve and go a long way toward adding appeal. There is the tendency with student animators to push these too far, and that can create a very rubber-hose look, impacting the integrity of the anatomy of the character. That may be desirable in situations where the design of the character or the style of animation supports that, but with most animation, even broad, cartoony animation, use these controls sensibly, as a means to sweeten the pose.

3.10 *Despicable Me*, **2010**
Gru's beautifully silhouetted pose is also a great study in straight against curve and its subtle use to add appeal to the pose.

Simple against Complex

The aforementioned proud pose is a stationary example of this idea; however, more often than not we see the idea of simple against complex played out more clearly when the character is in motion. When in motion, the leading edge of a character is likely to be a cleaner and simpler line due to the fact that many of the body parts will be dragging behind, creating a more complicated trailing edge. Whether the character is in motion or completely still, applying this principle of design, where appropriate, can plus the pose, making it more appealing.

Similar to the idea of contrasting shapes within the body of a character using straight against curve, "simple against complex" describes the outer edge of a shape or group of shapes. If your character is proudly poised, chest out, head and arms back, they are likely to have a nice simple curve that describes the overall shape of the front of their body. The opposite side of the character will have more detail and be more complex as the arms, head, and other shapes comprise the back side of the character.

3.11 *Madagascar 3: Europe's Most Wanted*, 2012
A continuous line of action can be clearly seen running through both Marty and Gia. Also take note of the simple leading edge running along the front of the characters, contrasting with the more complex shapes trailing behind.

Line of Action

3.12

3.12 *Despicable Me*, 2010
An S curve line of action can be seen running through Vector, Gru's nemesis, as he reclines in his lair.

The line of action is the invisible line that runs through the character, giving it an overall feeling of movement and connectedness. So much can be communicated with just a simple line. For instance, let's start with a straight line. If the line of action is perfectly vertical, it can make the character appear rigid and immovable. However, if that character is being launched into space, there's a whole lot of movement but at the same time, the body can be perfectly rigid. The same goes for a horizontal line. The character could either be moving really fast, as if shot from a cannon, or completely still, lying prone on the floor—yet rigid in both extremes. A diagonal line, by contrast, usually implies motion, as it's inherently unstable, leaning, giving a sense of being off balance. And that's all from just a simple straight line. For most poses, however, the line of action will be curvilinear, revealing points of relaxation and tension in different parts of the body. In general, you'll want the line of action to be simple, usually in a C or S shape, and you'll want to avoid sharp changes in direction, as that interrupts the flow of the line, making the pose feel disjointed.

After you've established the line of action, creating an exaggerated pose becomes an easy task, as you can simply make the line more extreme by pushing the arc of the line. Conversely, you can dial it back to make the pose more subtle and contained. I will typically push the pose much further than necessary, and I often find myself having to tone things down quite a bit. The main reason I do this is that if I can clearly see the line of action, it becomes much easier to construct the pose around that, creating that sense of movement and connectedness through the pose. If I have to make changes, I find it easier to pull the pose back than to have to push it afterward. In practice, since the line of action is the foundation of the pose, I'll start with the main body control and have it match that line of action as much as possible. Then, I'll work outward from there, creating the curve of the spine and the tilt of the head, and continue to build on top of that.

Head, Shoulders, Knees, and Toes

In the previous sections, we discussed some overall design principles to consider when creating your poses. We'll now go into some specifics as to how to pose the different parts of the body.

The Spine

Since the line of action runs through and, to a large degree, represents the curve of the spine, you can base the rotation of the hips and torso on this same line, by rotating them perpendicular to this line. Because of this, the torso and the hips are usually at odds with each other, rotated in opposite directions. For instance, if your hips are tilted up with the left side rotated forward, the torso is usually tilted down and the left side rotated backward. If you can find the rotation of one, you can easily determine the rotation of the other. It's as easy as that! The Italians came up with a fancy word to describe this: *contrapposto. Contrapposto* simply means "counterpose."

So do the hips and torso always counter each other? For the most part, they do. There are, of course, exceptions to this general rule. If your spine is forming an S curve instead of the more common C curve, the angle of the torso and hips are more likely to match each other. And this serves as a reminder that with any technique, you don't want to apply it blindly. You're not a mindless button masher—you're an artist—so use your ever-developing eye to make good choices.

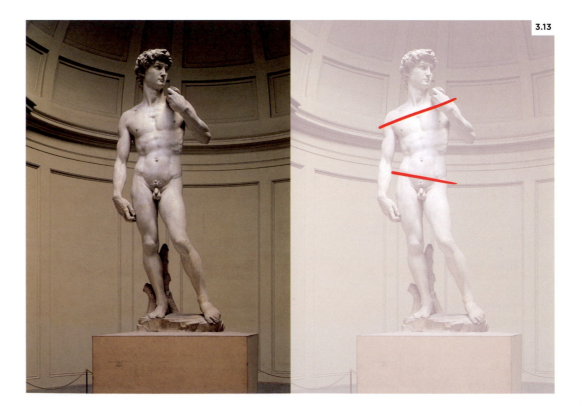

3.13

3.13 *David*, **Michelangelo Buonarroti, 1501–1504**
The statue of David is a wonderful example of contrapposto, where the hips and torso are rotated in opposite directions, adding a sense of weight to the pose.

3.14

The Head

The head can be in alignment with the line of action or it can often counter it, to add a bit of contrast and balance to the pose. Most of the rotation of the head is where the base of the head meets the top of the neck, not at the base of the neck. At the base of the neck, most of the movement is constrained to a forward/backward movement. Feel free to rotate your own head and neck around and discover the range of movement. In cartoony animation, we do have the freedom to break things, but there should be some respect for the anatomy to ground our characters in reality. It's a good thing to be mindful of the range of motion that our own bodies are capable of. This especially holds true in our pose test, where we're holding on a pose. If the character looks broken in a held pose, that's a bit of a problem, as the audience is going to notice. It's in the breakdowns where we can break the anatomy, and that's another story, one we'll get to in Chapter 4.

3.14 *Horton Hears a Who!*, 2008
In this still, Mayor Ned McDodd's head is tilted back and slightly to one side, contrasting the angle of his torso. Notice, too, how almost all of this rotation is happening at the base of the head.

3.15

The Shoulders

The shoulders are often ignored, but they shouldn't be. The shoulders are the eyebrows of the body. Reread that last sentence again and stare off into the distance, contemplating the meaning and significance of that statement. I wish I could give proper credit to whoever coined this because I think it's absolutely brilliant. How the shoulders are posed can communicate so much about what the character is feeling. Shoulders can show whether a character is relaxed or tense. They can show when a character is feeling uncertain, as in a shrugging motion, or if a character

is feeling apprehensive and shy. They can communicate rage when they're sharply raised—or nonchalance or complacency when they're drooped. As you can see, they're an important consideration when creating your poses. They usually work together, in sync with one another, and the primary motion is up and down. They can move forward or backward, but that's typically only used when the arms are angled sharply in the same direction, to avoid pinching at the base of the arm. Don't ignore the shoulders. Remember, *the shoulders are the eyebrows of the body.*

3.15 *Kung Fu Panda*, 2008
All the characters in this image from *Kung Fu Panda* have their shoulders raised to show their alertness—except the snake for obvious, anatomical reasons. Notice how the shoulders are working together in tandem with each other, which is usually the case.

3.16 *Hotel Transylvania*, **2012**
Dracula strikes a pose that incorporates a variety of good design choices that create appeal. Notice the arms and the line of action that runs through both of them, creating a feeling of connectedness and flow.

Arms and Legs

For the arms and legs, chances are the line of action is carried through one or both of them, so it's a no brainer how to pose them. In situations where that's not the case, what's been extremely helpful to me is the concept of flow, something I learned in figure drawing classes. When we think of flow, we naturally think of water. And when water is flowing, it likes to continue down the path of least resistance. How that translates into posing is that you'll want to avoid a disjointed look when posing the limbs. That doesn't mean that you can't have a sharp change in direction. The elbows and knees are joints that are frequently angled sharply. The same thing holds true with water, where it can turn sharply based on its environment. However, there's resistance there. A sharp angle creates tension and that can be desired and perfectly appropriate at times. It's more of a gestalt approach, where the sum of the parts should be harmonious and in support of each other. Working this way produces a feeling of connectedness, where the body parts are all working together.

This idea is clearly demonstrated in the poses of ballet dancers. If this is all too touchy-feely, go back to the more masculine idea of a line of action! There can be more than one line of action. For instance, you can have a line of action that goes through both arms. It's the same idea, where there's a flow that courses through the body with all the parts connected and working together, in peace, love, and harmony.

Wrists and Ankles

Like the arms and legs, the concept
of flow can be applied here as well,
especially when dealing with a pose
that has a more loose and relaxed feel.
In situations where you want to counter
that flow, adding tension or contrast,
my main suggestion would be to respect
the anatomy of the character to avoid a
broken look and feel.

Examine your own wrist, for example.
We can rotate our wrists considerably
along the same axis as the forearm and
we can also tilt our wrists up and down
to around 90 degrees. But when we tilt
the wrist side to side, most of us max
out at around 30 degrees either way.
Anything much more than that can give
a broken look. The same goes for ankles.
Look at your own ankles to examine the
range of motion. I see broken ankles
quite frequently in student work,
especially when a character is crouching
down and the feet are flat on the ground
with the ankles hyperextended well past
90 degrees, the physical limit we see in
most people. In those cases, the ball of
the foot should be rotated to help bear
the weight.

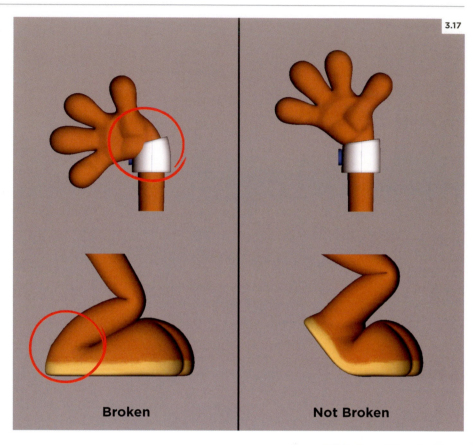

3.17

Broken   **Not Broken**

3.17 Broken wrists and ankles
Here we see some examples of
broken wrists and ankles. We
should respect the anatomy
when posing out the character.
That being said, during quick
transitions and fast action, all
bets are off.

3.18 *Hotel Transylvania*, 2012
Quasimodo Wilson's left hand is wonderfully expressive, if not a bit contorted in this still. Contrast that with the elegance of Dracula's fingers on Jonathan's shoulders.

Fingers and Toes

Last, but certainly not least, we get to the fingers and toes. For the love of humanity, avoid at all costs Ping-Pong paddle hands. What's this? It's the default pose for a hand where the fingers are straight out, resembling a Ping-Pong paddle. I see this all the time in student work and it's maddening! Take a moment and look around you. If no one is around, look at your own hands. Notice anything? They're never in a bad pose. Hands always look awesome in real life. Always. There's usually a nice gentle curve to the bend of the fingers. And the fingers are seldom all grouped together, bent the same amount. Usually there's a tapering-off effect where the forefinger is the straightest of the bunch and the pinky is the most curved.

Hands are very important. They're super expressive and communicate a lot about how the person is feeling, but they're so often ignored in animation and treated as secondary citizens. I think part of this is because they're rather difficult and time consuming to pose. I get this. There are usually more controls in the hands than are in the rest of the body, so it takes a while to pose them. Seeing as how the pose test should be executed rather quickly, the hands tend to be left alone until after an initial buy-off from the director. However, at the very least, grab all the finger controls and add a gentle, relaxed curve to the fingers to avoid Ping-Pong paddle hands.

3.19

The Face

This book is primarily concerned with pantomime acting and body action, so we won't be going into facial performance and lip-sync. However, it's worth mentioning it in regard to cartoony animation. A lot of facial animation is created using the layered approach—where the eyes are animated first, then the brows, then the jaw open/close, then the mouth corners, and so on. This makes sense, and it is how I usually approach facial animation.

However, there's something to be said about using a pose-based approach, especially when it comes to the principle of squash and stretch. When the brows are furrowed and eyes squinted,

creating a squashed appearance in the top half of the face, it makes good sense to compress the lower half of the face as well, raising the jaw, tightening the lips, and pushing out the cheeks to create a face that's squashed as a whole. This gives you some place to go—meaning, you can then transition into surprised, raised brows, jaw dropped look, sharply contrasting the prior pose. That's a rather extreme example, but you can use a much more subtle approach when dealing with just dialogue. The *m* or *b* sound, for example, is a great one to consider squashing the whole face on, to a much smaller degree. Usually the following sound will allow you to stretch the face, again subtly, to give the facial animation a fleshier feel overall.

3.19 *Cloudy with a Chance of Meatballs 2,* **2013**
With the exception of the strawberry and cameraman, the faces in this image are subtly stretched, adding to the characters' sense of awe at what they're seeing.

SCENE PREP

DESIGNING
THE POSE

A PRINCIPLED
ANIMATION

INTERVIEW:
MATT WILLIAMES

STEP-BY-STEP
WALKTHROUGH

OVER TO YOU!

A PRINCIPLED ANIMATION

We'll now take a brief look at the principles of animation that specifically pertain to cartoony animation and talk about how they can be applied.

Anticipation

The primary definition of anticipation is that you're communicating to the audience what's going to happen next. Anticipation is usually manifested in a smaller movement in the opposite direction before the main movement—like a weight shift over the left leg before taking a step with the right. However, in the case of an angry bull, it could be his pawing the ground before he charges horns-first toward a taunting troubadour. In both these cases, the intent of the character is displayed, where the former deals more with the physical movement and the latter deals more with the thought process.

When it comes to cartoony animation, we're mostly concerned with the physical movement that precedes the main action. This can be broken down into three different aspects: time, magnitude, and amount. With regard to time, generally speaking, the faster the main movement is, the longer you'll want to anticipate. Think of it in terms of building up energy. Like an arrow that's pulled back in a bow, the longer the character is wound up, the quicker we expect him to move afterward. To go to an extreme, you can even have the character disappear from the screen entirely, but give the impression that he launched off in a certain direction, if you anticipate long enough in the opposite direction. You can't just have them disappear from the screen—you'll usually want to have some motion lines or dry-brush to create a blurred effect. We'll go over those kinds of techniques in Chapter 6.

When thinking about how broad the anticipation or the magnitude of the move should be, it follows the same general rule that the magnitude of movement for the anticipation should be appropriately matched to the magnitude of the main movement. However, there are exceptions to any generality, and you can have a lot of fun playing with the magnitude of an anticipation. For instance, if you have a character wildly anticipate a run but then start off at a crawling pace, comedy can come from breaking that expectation.

3.20

Mayor Shelbourne's arm is extended out and his head is tilted back in anticipation of downing all three burgers in one bite.

Lastly, we get to the amount of anticipation to use. Can you anticipate an anticipation, for instance? Yes, you can! If a character is going to jump upward, you could have him rise a little on the balls of his feet before the main anticipation of crouching down. You can even anticipate an anticipation of an anticipation to an anticipation. Although most moves will have only one or two anticipations, you can have a lot of fun by playing around with how many to use. All that being said, another thing to consider is that not every move needs an anticipation. If you mindlessly apply an anticipation to every move, your animation will quickly become formulaic and uninteresting. A head turn, for example, doesn't always have to have an anticipation. A simple slow-out and slow-in will sometimes suffice.

A common formula I see in student work for most moves is to anticipate in the opposite direction, drop the hips during the breakdown, overshoot the final pose, and then settle. This formula gets repeated for every move and creates a predictable and boring performance. Think before you anticipate and be inventive. Always ask yourself how fast (time), how much (magnitude), and how many (amount) with regard to anticipations, and you'll be better equipped to deliver entertaining choices.

Exaggeration

Exaggeration is one of the hallmarks that separates animation from live action. As an animator, our calling is to make the unbelievable believable, and exaggeration is one of the ways we can do this. When we think of exaggeration, we tend to think that it means to make things bigger and broader. This is especially true in cartoony animation where characters that are excited by what they're seeing can have their eyeballs literally pop out of their heads. This understanding is plain enough. But exaggeration can also mean the opposite, where instead of going to an extreme pushed pose, we can make the character completely

still and with just an eye dart, get much more mileage out of the gag. Think of it this way: if everything is important, then nothing is important. Likewise, if everything is exaggerated, then nothing is exaggerated. We should strive for a degree of contrast so that those heightened moments have significance.

So how do you exaggerate a pose? If you're going for big, as I mentioned earlier in the chapter, finding the line of action is key. If you can see it, you can push it. Be fearless with your posing, and see just how far you can push things. On the opposite end of the exaggeration spectrum, experiment

with just how little you can move things to see if that is a better choice. Remember, not everything should be grand, as contrast is what makes things interesting. More importantly, keep in mind that exaggeration should always be motivated by the character and/or story. Exaggerating for the sake of exaggeration can lead to a soulless display of one's skill. Always remember your work is in service of the story and, ultimately, the audience.

3.21 *Hotel Transylvania*, 2012
In this frame we see a nice contrast between an exaggeratedly broad pose on the suit of armor and an exaggeratedly contained pose with Dracula.

3.21

Squash and Stretch

Nothing says cartoony action like squash and stretch. And in the land of cartoons, as long as the character design supports it, we can squash and stretch to our hearts' content. On a technical note, the main limitation I see with computer animation is when the rig is not designed to squash and stretch. Recent rigging techniques have opened up the possibility to incorporate it, and it's only going to get better as the demand for flexible rigs increases.

When applying squash and stretch, it's important to note that we usually don't want to hold the pose on an extreme squash or stretch. The very nature of squash and stretch is that there are forces at play, causing the character to deform. Think of a bouncing ball. It stretches as it nears the ground, going at high speed. Velocity and friction cause it to form an elongated shape. Upon impact, this causes the pent up energy to be displaced laterally, as it can no longer travel in the downward direction. In both those cases, the ball is only squashed or stretched for just a few frames—not enough for the human eye to take in the image. It's more felt than seen. And again, in that example, it's also important to note that the ball should maintain volume, that when it's stretched, the ball will get skinnier around the middle section and likewise, when squashed, will bulge out as the shape becomes more compressed. Most rigs will account for this automatically. However, it's always nice to have the freedom to control the amount of squash and stretch manually, and more advanced rigs will support this.

The one important exception to maintaining volume is when creating a smear frame. In that case, volume is not maintained, as the character is smeared across the frame, simulating the motion blur inherent in live-action filmmaking. We'll dive into smear frames in greater detail in Chapter 6, as it's an important and specific type of stretching. So when creating your pose test, if it's a static pose and not an extreme anticipation or fast action, apply squash and stretch subtly. You don't want to make the character look distorted in those moments where there are no extreme forces working on them. However, when creating those fast actions and hard impacts, make liberal use of this wonderful principle of animation. It'll give your character a fleshy, lively feel and greatly enhance the cartooniness of the animation.

3.22 Squashed
Recent advances in rigging are giving computer animators greater control over squash and stretch, something the 2D guys have had from the very beginning.

3.22

Timing (and Spacing)

Spacing isn't one of the 12 principles of animation, though its importance is often overlooked. I didn't even hear about spacing until I was a couple of years into the industry, and this was after four years of animation school! This may have been because at that time traditional animation concepts were just starting to infiltrate my computer animation workflow. So why am I talking about spacing in a section devoted to timing? Because timing and spacing are closely linked. They're not the same thing, however, and the distinction between the two can be confusing at first. Simply put, timing is how many frames it takes for something to move, and spacing is the amount of distance traveled between those frames. I doubt that did much to clear up any confusion, so it's probably more helpful to look at the illustration 3.22 below. Timing for cartoony animation is generally quicker than more naturalistic animation. Tex Avery and Bob Clampett,

two early Warner Bros. directors, clearly distinguished themselves from the more soft slow-in and slow-out approach common in Disney films by having their characters zip across the screen—sometimes in just a frame or two. Although this broad generalization holds true in the more extreme examples, cartoony "timing" is equally a result of how you adjust the spacing.

For instance, in the animated example we're looking at in this book, Mr. Buttons does a quick take, a reaction to what he sees when the door is opened. In terms of timing, after the anticipation, there will likely be a 16-frame jump into the air. If I were to animate in and out of those extremes with a gentle slow-out and slow-in, it probably wouldn't look very cartoony at all. However, by changing the spacing to where there's a fast-out of the anticipation, with broad spacing that then slows-in tightly into the jump pose, I've created a much

more cartoony feel by adjusting the spacing. The timing is the same—it's the spacing that makes the difference. We'll dive more into spacing when we talk about breakdowns, but for now, as you start creating your poses for the pose test, don't worry too much about the timing and whether or not it's cartoony enough. One of computer animation's strengths is that we can change the timing very easily by dragging the keys around the timeline. Without fail, as we start adding in the breakdowns, our keyframes will continually be shifted around until we find the right timing in between the actions.

3.23 Spacing
If you look carefully at these two examples, you'll notice that both of the balls have the exact same timing. By simply adjusting the spacing, you can completely change the feel of the motion, making it cartoonier.

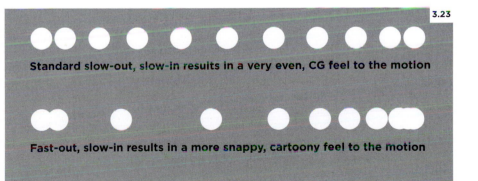

3.23

Standard slow-out, slow-in results in a very even, CG feel to the motion

Fast-out, slow-in results in a more snappy, cartoony feel to the motion

MATT WILLIAMES

Matt Williames is a traditional animator who has worked on feature films for Warner Bros., Disney, and DreamWorks. He also animated on the short film, *Adam and Dog* (2011), which was nominated for an Oscar and won an Annie award for Best Animated Short Subject. He recently started animating in CG, so I spoke with Matt to get his thoughts on character animation and about his foray into computer animation.

How do you approach animating a character for the first time? What do you do to get into the character's head?

For me, it usually starts with the director. If the director has a really strong vision of what they want, I'm just trying to get into that headspace and that world. So I feel like that's the key to unlocking everything in terms of your success of animating a character. With a director that doesn't seem to have a very clear vision, in some ways, I kind of like it, because it means I get to make up my own mind on the character, get a feel for tone of the film, and using lots and lots of reference. But overall, I'm trying to get in on the ground floor of understanding what the director wants, see how the character fits in context to the story, and then making choices from there, from an acting standpoint. Once you get all that stuff settled, which takes a few shots, things start to fall in line.

What's your planning process? Do you do thumbnails, video reference, or some other process?

Yeah, that's a good question. I know the answer I'm supposed to give is that I thumbnail, scrupulously, but I really don't thumbnail a whole lot. I know, for me, it really ruins that sense of spontaneity that I want to save for when I'm animating. And that's the thing that always amazes me about people that do thumbnails all the time. The ones that do it and their work still feels spontaneous—I'm always impressed by that.

Having said that, I do plan in my head. I'm one of these guys that has to see it really clearly, you know? If I don't see it, I can't draw. I'm not like a Glen Keane, who feels an emotion and can draw based on that feeling, cause Glen doesn't see drawings, he feels the feeling and then draws. I can feel a feeling, but if I don't see it, I can't draw it. So I have to really visualize.

I really do map out my shots in my head, with just a couple main drawings. And as long as I have those main poses, then I can work on how I'm going to get in and out of those poses and what I'm going to do in terms of business. So I like to have that sort of fence to keep me in the boundary of, this is what the shot's about, but then have freedom within that to improvise and to find those little funny character quirks and traits.

It's almost like the difference between Meisner and Stanislavski, where Stanislavski is all about method acting—it's all about putting your own experience onto the character, so if you've actually had a family member die, then the character's experiencing that moment. You're putting that experience onto the character. So you're thinking of your grandmother, when that character is maybe thinking of their sister or something like that. Whereas with Meisner, you're so in the moment that it just comes out naturally. And it's funny how you can really see the difference in the performance, and the choices you make are completely different in those two different states. And I found that to be true when I thumbnail. It's like the method approach for me, like Stanislavski, where I'm putting my own experiences on top. But I have to be careful because it's not my experience, it's the character's, and I'm not the character.

So then there's another part of me where I take that sort of loose guideline, and then I just have to be in the moment. So that's when roughing out a shot, you just can't be bothered, but you really have to have focus because that's where all the really cool magic happens that you never ever plan. So for me, that's kind of how I approach it. And it's always different for every shot too, I have to say. If it's something I've never done before, sometimes I will thumbnail more than I normally would, just because I don't even know how to start planning in my head. And sometimes seeing a drawing can make me go, oh, okay, this is a starting point. But I'd say 90 percent of the time I don't thumbnail.

I had the pleasure of working alongside you when you were still getting your feet wet in CG. What was the experience like?
I like CG when it embraces the medium that it is. And I don't mean by being hyper-real, I just mean by doing what it's good at doing. And I don't want to put it in a box and say that that's all it can do, because any art form is limitless in its own way. Personally, I just enjoy animating with hand-drawn animation more. For me, when I was doing some CG, I've always felt a disconnect between me and the character. And it was weird, because when I finished my first shot in CG, I remember seeing it after it was rendered and lit, and I remember expecting to feel this sense of ownership, especially since it never went through another artist's hands, and it came up and it played and I felt nothing. I just felt nothing.

So, what do you think would help bridge that? Is it the tools? Is it just that it's inside the computer?
I'm just a very tactile person. Even in hand-drawn animation, I don't like using a tablet and traditional animation software because there's something to me about the magic that is drawing on a piece of paper. With computer animation, it's the feeling that I've never touched the character. But I love that a lot of CG films have hand drawn people working on them, so that sensibility is getting out there more and more. But with hand-drawn animation, you really are a designer; even if you didn't design the character there's nothing stopping you from making a really nice drawing. With CG, if you can't pose it, you can't do it and you're out of luck if the arms don't reach the top of the head.

There are some creative things that you could do to try and cheat it, but you can only cheat so far before it just breaks the rig. So it always frustrated me that I could never get that truly graphic nature of hand drawn into my CG as much as I had hoped. So I think that was definitely part of it, but I honestly think there's something about flipping paper, about how there was nothing on those pages until I drew it. And so it's literally like you're birthing this creation, and when it's done you really do feel a sense of ownership to it. I don't know how else to compare it. I don't dislike CG, and I think there's some really neat stuff coming out. I love that Disney's going back to its roots a little bit, in terms of trying to fight for appealing designs and characters in their animation. But no, I don't truly dislike it, I just don't love it the way I love hand-drawn animation.

Yeah, I think there's this encouraging trend that it's not about posing the character—it's about designing the pose, and I always found that kind of fascinating. I guess, from your perspective, having that sense of design, having the ability to draw something appealing but not being able to apply that aesthetic directly onto the CG character—that that was a source of frustration.

Yeah, to get by that I would pose out the character, and then, when I was really getting into refining the expressions, I would always get a draw tool out, and just draw on top of it. I had a really hard time taking an existing model that had this blank expression, pushing and pulling and doing stuff like that, trying to get what I wanted. I could sort of get it, but then I would just draw on top of it. The cool thing is that your drawing stays there and the puppet remains interactive—you could just match it right with that eyelid and then shape it to that.

You've also taught animation at CalArts. Having worked with students, and also working as a professional in animation, what advice do you have for students looking to enter the field? How do they differentiate themselves in this highly competitive industry?
That's a really tough one because it completely starts with the student's own sensibilities. One thing I see is that there are just a lot of fans in animation. I think we really have to take a step back and really look at ourselves. We all love Glen Keane and love what he has to say about

being an artist, but are we really doing that? I mean, are we genuinely looking at film as an art form, as opposed to popular culture? And I know that the big thing is: Is it entertaining? But what does that really mean?

When I think of entertaining in the way that they mean it, I think of a theatre full of people laughing. And that's not at all, like, for me, what entertaining could mean. A haiku is not what I would call entertaining, but it's high art, and it's a lot of abstract thought going on there, and that's completely valid. So I guess all I'm saying is to really delve into film as an art form. And I think that your choices are going to change because of that, because it's not just a matter of watching some Woody Allen films or films by Sofia Coppola, or Terrence Malick—but it's more about figuring out why did they make the film the way they made it? And if you don't understand it, watch it again, and really analyze it. And I think when you start to look into that world of film, you start to see things really differently.

When it comes to acting, in animation, all the acting is kind of the same. There is a moment in one of

Robert De Niro's films—*Goodfellas*, I think—where he is reacting to something really traumatic. And he doesn't react! He just stares and doesn't do anything. With that character, it was all internal. When thinking about his reaction, or lack of one, it's really getting to the core of why he made that choice. And I feel like that's what's missing by and large in a lot of student work. On *Adam and Dog*, there were a lot of moments where we didn't overexplain, and that was very intentional. I remember, somebody criticized the dog, saying he wasn't sure what the dog's personality was, and I was like, whoa, whoa, whoa, you're coming at it from a completely different paradigm. You're thinking of this like a Disney film. This is just a real dog. He doesn't really have thoughts and feelings, he's just following Adam around because Adam was created in the image of God, and there's something different about this guy than all the other animals in the forest, in the garden. And so that's all there is going on there, and there's something very sweet and subtle about that. So I feel like when people start to break out from the norm, you see that different spark coming into their work.

I like CG when it embraces the medium that it is. And I don't mean by being hyper-real, I just mean by doing what it's good at doing.
MATT WILLIAMES

STEP-BY-STEP WALKTHROUGH

In this walkthrough, I'll be building one of the poses for the animation from the ground up, detailing the process as I go along. Pretty much every pose I create follows the same thought process and is executed in the same way. One thing I try to do when moving on to the next pose is to reset the rig so that I'm building my extreme poses from scratch. There are exceptions to this, as when animating a series of poses that are similar, where there are only slight changes from one extreme to another. In that case, I find that it's good practice to build on the previous pose.

For most broad action, resetting the pose can prevent problems like the dreaded gimbal lock we discussed earlier. Rotating a control that already has high rotational values is a surefire way to wind up in gimbal hell. It may take a little longer to construct each pose from the ground up but you'll be better off for it in the end. Along

the same lines, it's important to work cleanly, making sure that you're not using different controls that are affecting the same area on the rig. For instance, if you're translating the head around, it's not good practice to also rotate the base of the neck. Both controls achieve the same result. Now you've got rotations on top of translations on two separate controls, and it becomes difficult to sort through that when you start refining the motion.

If you're tracking the arc on a nose, for instance, and the motion is full of hitches, either one of those controls could be causing the problem, and it will be difficult to track down. It's the same thing with the shoulders. If they can be both translated and rotated, pick one and stick with it. Keeping things clean at this stage is critical, as you want to build a solid foundation for your animation and avoid as many future headaches as possible.

The Anticipation Pose

The pose I'll be building will be the anticipation pose he goes into before coming to a stop at the front door of his blind date's house. I'll be using Figure 3.24, the thumbnail drawing from my planning, as the basis for this pose, keeping in mind that this is a fluid process and that creating an exact copy of the thumbnail is not the goal. It's more important that I capture the idea and the feeling of the pose rather than let my sketch dictate what I do. There's also a good chance that I'll be dealing with limitations in the rig that will necessitate some flexibility on my part when trying to capture the essence of the pose.

3.24

3.24 Anticipation pose

1. First things first—I need to find the line of action (see Figure 3.25). Since I'll be building the pose from the core of the character outward, finding this is critical. Since I built this thumbnail drawing around the line of action, finding it was pretty straightforward. If you're having difficulty locating the line of action in a thumbnail drawing or video reference, the overall curvature of the spine will reveal it. Don't worry about getting the pose perfectly right. Through the process of posing the character rig, you'll inevitably return to previous parts of the character you've already moved or rotated, tweaking and refining them to strengthen the pose.

2. The first control you'll want to move and rotate will be the main body control. Different rigs have different names for this control. Some rigs call it the COG (Center of Gravity). Others will call it the body control or something else entirely. Regardless of how it's named, it's the control that drives the entirety of the character, with the exception of the IK hands and feet. Select this control and try to match the line of action of the pose (see Figure 3.26). Granted, it's going to appear rather stiff but we'll add the curvature of the spine in the next step.

3. Moving outward from there, let's pose the spine of the character, rotating the controls to better match the line of action. In most rigs, you can pose the spine using FK or IK controls. Some animators can be pretty staunch proponents of one type over another. Ignore them. Whatever works for you is the best choice. When posing the spine, don't forget about *contrapposto*, and make sure the hips and torso are angled opposite to each other (see Figure 3.27).

3.25 **Finding the line of action**

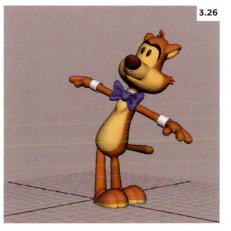

3.26 **Matching the line of action**

3.27 **Posing the spine**

4. Since Mr. Buttons will be looking in the direction he's about to go, I'll rotate his head in the opposite direction to his body (see Figure 3.28). This also adds tension, giving the pose a wound-up feel that is appropriate for the action that will follow. He's going to quickly spring out of this anticipation pose, so whatever we can do to build up the tension is a good thing.

5. Up until this point, things have been pretty straightforward. However, I'm noticing in my thumbnail (Figure 3.24) that I didn't fully think things through. For starters, the foot that's planted on the ground is facing the wrong direction. It should be pointed in the same direction he's traveling (see Figure 3.29). And second, I realize I should switch the feet around so that the foot that's in the air should cross over the one that's on the ground. Just as with the head, this adds to the feeling that he's winding up like a tight spring. I'm also switching his feet around because, in the pose that follows, I'd like for him to be as untwisted as possible when going into the smear. No pose exists in a vacuum, so I need to be mindful of what precedes and what follows. Changing things up like this happens all the time, so remaining flexible when making your pose test is key.

6. I really wanted to stay true to the silhouette of the thumbnail when dealing with his arms. Because his head is fairly huge, I ended up having to break the rig, translating his shoulder high enough to give some negative space around it. It's not visible to the main camera so I did what I needed to do to get the pose (see Figure 3.30). Because of the size of his head, I'm sure this will not be the only time I have to do this—something to keep in mind when working with this character. Also, because the tips of his fingers are rather bulbous, when I curled them in to make a fist, there was some geometry penetration going on. Again, much of this is hidden from the camera so it's not a big deal. When I go in to polish the animation, I'll be double-checking to make sure any cheats like this aren't visible. For now, I'm not going to get too caught up in details as there's always the chance big changes will occur during the early stages of the animation process.

3.28 Posing the head

3.29 Posing the legs and feet

3.30 Posing the arms and hands

7. Normally, I'd leave the tail alone as it's primarily going to be a floppy bit—something that gets dragged along for the ride. But something about it being perfectly rigid draws attention to itself. And there's a good chance the director will mention it as well. For now, I'll quickly pose it out, realizing that I'll have to redo it later when the animation is more fleshed out (see Figure 3.31).

8. During the pose test, I'll frequently animate only the eye-line of the character just so he's not staring straight off into space (see Figure 3.32). I do this because I figure if I can communicate the intent of the character purely through body language, I've done my job and adding facial animation will only plus this. The other reason is that it can take a while to pose the face, and there's a good chance I'll be scrapping much of what I initially pose out. I don't want to spend a lot of time on something, getting married to it, if it's going to be tossed out. Typically, I'll add in facial poses and lip-sync after I've gotten an initial buy-off from the director—which usually occurs after the breakdown phase (see Chapter 4). For the sake of this demo, I'll add in the facial pose now. The eyes, easy enough, will be looking where he's heading. For the rest of the face, I've played with some squash and stretch, squashing the right side of his face and stretching his left side, the direction he's looking. This will give his face a fleshier feel while also adding asymmetry and appeal.

9. Like facial, I'll usually save finessing the pose until the director is happy with the direction I'm headed. But once I've gotten that buy-off, I'll go in and sweeten the pose, using secondary controls to add minute bends to the arms and legs, tweaking the overall shapes to make them more appealing (see Figure 3.33). Notice the subtle changes to the shape of his head, for instance. The raised foot also has a curvature to it. These modifications, while slight, go a long way toward adding appeal. I'll also be addressing some of the secondary parts of the character, like the hairs on his head, his ears, and his bowtie, things I've ignored until now. Giving this kind of attention and love to every pose, and ultimately every frame, will help set your work apart and make it frame-by-frame worthy.

3.31 Posing the tail

3.32 Posing the face

3.33 Finessing the pose

IT'S TIME TO ANIMATE!

If you haven't already done so, take Mr. Buttons and start getting familiar with the rig. Every rig is different, and there's always a ramp-up period before you start cruising.

There is documentation along with the rig to help you get started. But before you start your shot, remember your scene prep:

1. Reference in the rig and any other assets you need for your scene.

2. Create your select-all shelf button.

3. Create your camera, place it in position, and lock it so you're animating to that camera.

4. After that, start constructing poses, following my example.

This book covers only the construction of one pose; however, like I mentioned earlier, I use the same process for every pose. So start posing!

You can animate the same or a similar shot, or you can try something entirely new. It's totally up to you.

CHAPTER FOUR
BREAKDOWNS

What is a breakdown? Simply put, it's breaking down the motion between two extremes. From a mechanical perspective, breakdowns primarily determine the overlapping action, the arcs that the parts of the body are moving along, and the slow-in or slow-out of that action. From a personality perspective, breakdowns can tell us a lot about the character. How a character moves between extremes is just as revealing as the poses themselves. For example, if a character leads the action with his head or chest, instead of his hips, it could be communicating that he's a type A personality—headstrong and confident.

Breakdowns are probably my favorite thing to create because that's where the fun happens, especially in regard to cartoony animation. Techniques like smears, motion lines, and multiple limbs are primarily used during the breakdowns, where the action is fast enough to justify their use. Breakdowns are also fun to create because we can explore many different ways to break down an action—the possibilities are endless.

LIKING WHAT YOU GET VERSUS GETTING WHAT YOU LIKE

"Liking what you get" is what can happen when you let Maya do the work for you. If you don't create breakdowns and change your tangents into spline with just your pose test, unless you have a well-developed eye, you may accept what you see and move on. This inevitably leads to swimmy transitions where there's evenness to the movement, giving it a very computery feel. Going spline too soon can completely obscure the great poses you just made. It can also create a lot of headaches down the line, as you'll now have to work harder to recapture the spark of life you created in the pose test. Creating our own breakdowns, taking the reigns away from Maya, reverses the order, moving us from liking what we get to getting what we like. Before we dive into what goes into a breakdown, let's look at some practices that can help us come closer to "getting what we like."

4.1 *Ice Age: The Meltdown*, **2006**
Sid the sloth is clearly leading with his hips in this breakdown pose, not only adding contrast and texture to the move but also revealing his playful attitude.

4.1

LIKING WHAT YOU
GET VS GETTING
WHAT YOU LIKE

BUILDING
A BETTER
BREAKDOWN

INTERVIEW:
PEPE SÁNCHEZ

STEP-BY-STEP
WALKTHROUGH

OVER TO YOU!

Four-Frame Rule

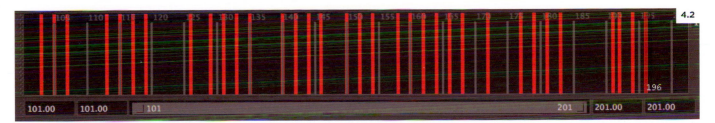

4.2 Keyframe timeline
Notice the keyframes in the timeline in our example animation and how they average out to roughly a keyframe every third frame. Notice, too, that I've broken the four-frame rule. I tend to tie my animation down probably more than I need to. The thing to keep in mind is to not let this "rule" dictate your workflow. Just use it as a guide.

How many breakdowns are enough? For simple transitions, quite often, one or two will do. For more complex actions, there may be as many as half a dozen or more. Remember, breakdowns are primarily used to define the arcs, the overlapping action, as well as the amount of slow-in and slow-out in the transition. So the amount of breakdowns will vary based on whether or not those conditions are adequately met. In general, a good rule of thumb is to have a keyframe, on average, every four frames. And by keyframe I mean both extremes and breakdowns. It's important to point out that this rule doesn't mean that you will have a keyframe on literally every fourth frame, where you've set a key on frames 4, 8, 12, 16, and so on. For a gentle slow-in to a pose, you may have a 12-frame gap between keyframes. For a fast,

complicated action, you may have one keyframe on every single frame through that transition. "On average" is the distinction. By working this way, things are tied down enough that you won't have a heart attack when you go spline.

It's also important to point out that every keyframe you set needs to have a purpose. Don't simply set keyframes for the sake of meeting this rule. There needs to be a reason for it to exist. Is it creating an extreme pose? Is it a breakdown pose? Is it defining an arc? Is it showing the amount of slow-in or slow-out to one extreme or another? Is it determining the overlapping action? We'll cover this in more detail soon enough, but keep in mind that every keyframe and breakdown should be created for a reason.

TweenMachine

We'll be creating our breakdowns with the help of Justin Barrett's tweenMachine tool. You can find the link to it on the companion website. The tweenMachine greatly expedites the process of creating an in-between pose, the foundation for a breakdown. It allows us to quickly key in a midway point between the extremes that we can then take and mold to our liking. We don't want to create our breakdowns from scratch. Even though Maya is the world's most ignorant inbetweener,

we can and should still use what Maya gives us for two important reasons. For one, it's a time saver, as it gives us something to work with instead of starting with a blank slate. And second, what Maya gives us is a mathematically precise transition pose between the two extremes and can ensure that our breakdowns are being built on solid footing. If you don't already have the tweenMachine installed, do so now, as the examples that follow will use this wonderful tool.

Page Flipping

When creating your breakdowns, using the page-flipping technique to visualize a breakdown is invaluable. You can page-flip, just like a traditional animator, by using the comma and period keys, allowing you to move back and forth in the timeline, from one keyframe to the next. This is far preferable to scrubbing through the timeline. For one reason, it's just quicker. This is especially useful if you've got a slow rig. And for another reason, if you're working in any tangent type besides stepped, page-flipping will simulate the look of stepped tangents by skipping any frames that don't have a keyframe on them. If you aren't already using these hotkeys, do yourself a favor and begin using them religiously. I firmly believe using them is vital to creating effective breakdowns.

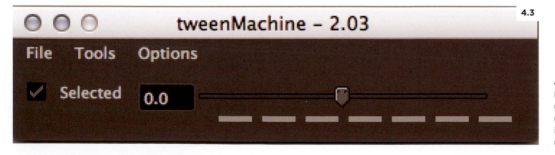

4.3

4.3 TweenMachine
Here's a screenshot of the ever useful tweenMachine. It may not be much to look at, but its functionality is a thing of matchless beauty.

LIKING WHAT YOU
GET VS GETTING
WHAT YOU LIKE

**BUILDING
A BETTER
BREAKDOWN**

INTERVIEW:
PEPE SÁNCHEZ

STEP-BY-STEP
WALKTHROUGH

OVER TO YOU!

BUILDING A BETTER BREAKDOWN

As mentioned earlier, from a mechanical perspective, we're primarily concerned with three things when creating a breakdown pose: arcs, slow-in and slow-out, and overlapping action. So let's look at each one in more detail.

Arcs, Opposing Arcs, and Path of Action

Arcs are one of the main things we're looking to add when creating a breakdown pose. They add beauty to our animation and give our characters lifelike motion. Anything natural moves in an arc. One way to sell a more mechanical, robotic movement is to eliminate arcs entirely. Arcs are also one of the keys to creating refined, polished motion, which we'll address in Chapter 5. As you can see, they're pretty important—important enough to be included in the esteemed 12 principles of animation.

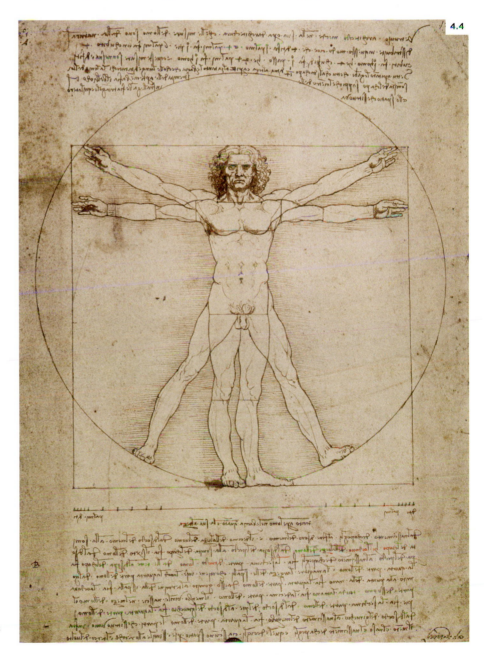

4.4

4.4 *The Vitruvian Man*
Leonardo Da Vinci's *The Vitruvian Man* is a study in human proportion. However, it also illustrates our bodies' construction and how our limbs move in arclike fashion.

Through careful observation of human movement, we realize that most actions originate from the hip, so I will usually look to incorporate an arc there when I first create my breakdown. Frequently, that arc will be a dipping action where the hip drops through the transition. However, dropping the hip is not to be thoughtlessly applied every single time. A character jumping is an obvious exception. However, since the force of gravity is always working against our character, arcing downward happens quite frequently. It's all a part of creating the illusion of weight in our character. Other parts of the character where you'll want to track the arcs are the wrists, ankles, and nose. Those are the more apparent places to look for an arc, and if there's an errant arc on one of those locations, it's rather obvious. Don't stop there, however. When you really start to fine-tune your animation, you'll even be looking to arc the corners of the mouth.

One thing to think about when creating arcs is looking for ways to oppose or counter them. If the hips are arcing down, perhaps an arm could be arcing upward. You don't want to force it, but if there's an opportunity to introduce opposing arcs and it looks natural, go for it! Doing so adds contrast to the action and can make it more dynamic and interesting.

Speaking of contrast, arcs can be simple or complex. Normally, when we think of an arc, we think of it as a simple line bowed in one direction. However, for some actions, arcs can change direction and get more complicated introducing twists and turns, depending on the complexity of the move. These more complicated arcs typically will happen at the extremities, like the wrists and the ankles. Take a walk cycle, for example. When a character is walking, the up and down movement of the hips will follow a relatively simple bouncing arc with each step. In the span of two steps, however, the wrists will follow a figure-of-eight pattern from the top view and, to a lesser extent, the side view. The further a body part is away from the core of the character, the more complicated the paths of action tend to become. Don't confuse path of action with line of action, however. The path of action is the arc that's created by tracking on a certain part of the body, whereas the line of action, as you may recall, is the invisible line running through the character. Even though the path of action can be complex at times, generally speaking, it should have a curvilinear, arcing quality to it.

Try not to get too caught up in how complex the arcs can get. Much of the time, they naturally develop as we build our breakdowns. The first place to start is almost always the hips, and once you have that arc defined, simply move out from there, hitting the primary arc-tracking points on the character: the wrists, ankles, and nose. As you page-flip between the extremes, be on the lookout for arcs and incorporate them into your breakdowns.

LIKING WHAT YOU
GET VS GETTING
WHAT YOU LIKE

BUILDING
A BETTER
BREAKDOWN

INTERVIEW:
PEPE SÁNCHEZ

STEP-BY-STEP
WALKTHROUGH

OVER TO YOU!

Slow-in, Slow-out

Since most of the time our characters are subject to the laws of physics, our transitions between extreme poses will usually have some degree of slow-in and slow-out. I say "most of the time" because in cartoon-land, as you know, we can have a lot of fun with breaking those laws. Nevertheless, for most actions, slow-in and slow-out should be incorporated into your breakdowns. Yet giving an equal amount of slow-in and slow-out for every action can cause your animation to become even-feeling and predictable.

To create some variety and contrast in your spacing, you can fast-out/slow-in or slow-out/fast-in. The former, fast-out/slow-in, is commonly seen in cartoony action where there's a quick

initial movement followed by a slow-in to a moving hold. I use this all the time, perhaps to a fault, when creating my breakdowns. The tweenMachine makes it easy to adjust your spacing this way by simply adjusting the slider to the left or the right when you create your breakdown.

Let's say you have your first extreme pose on frame 10 and your second extreme pose on frame 20 and are creating your breakdown at the midpoint, on frame 15. If you move the slider more to the left, you're favoring the first pose and the spacing will have a slow-out/fast-in feel, where the spacing is tighter at the beginning of the transition and broader toward the end. You can get the opposite effect, fast-out/

slow-in, by adjusting the slider toward the right. That being said, I usually start my breakdown at the halfway point, not favoring any one extreme or the other. By doing this, I can then use overlapping action to have different parts of the body moving at different speeds, creating a slow-out on some parts and a fast-out on others. This creates texture and complexity to the move and makes it more interesting. We'll look at overlapping action in a little more detail in the next section.

4.5 *Despicable Me*, 2010
Vector slows-in to Gru's side as he introduces himself. Most extreme poses will have some degree of slow-in and slow-out. In highly caricatured action, however, this principle is often dismissed for the sake of visual punch.

4.5

Overlapping Action and Reversals

4.6

4.6 *Rio*, **2011**
Nico and Pedro hover in flight. Frame-by-frame study of bird wings is a great way to observe overlapping action, where the feathers at the tip of the wing drag behind and overlap the base of the wing.

Overlapping action is where different parts of the body move at different rates of speed, breaking up the movement and making it more natural and fluid. As we discussed earlier, since most actions originate from the hip, this makes it fairly easy to determine what follows as we simply move outward from the body, delaying the other parts of the body.

If a pitcher is throwing a baseball, for example, the hips will anticipate backward, the upper body will stay behind, and the ball-throwing hand will be the last thing to settle into the glove. And that's just in the anticipation of the throw. When we animate out of the anticipation, again the hips lead, followed by the upper body with the arm staying behind before being catapulted toward home plate. Not everything is so simple, however, in that sometimes other parts of the body can lead the action. In that same example, let's say

that we broaden the action and the character pitches with such force that he's thrown off balance, and now the hips and feet are playing catch-up to prevent the character from falling. In that case, the ball-throwing hand, even though it was initially the last thing to move, has taken over as the primary force, causing the rest of the body to follow behind.

And while the hips often do lead the action, any part of the body can lead. This is especially true when it comes to external forces, like a baseball bat to the head. In that instance, the head is the first thing to move, followed in quick succession by the rest of the body. By playing with the idea of what parts of the body lead and arrive at different times, it can really liven up your animation and make it more dynamic and interesting.

LIKING WHAT YOU
GET VS GETTING
WHAT YOU LIKE

BUILDING
A BETTER
BREAKDOWN

INTERVIEW:
PEPE SÁNCHEZ

STEP-BY-STEP
WALKTHROUGH

OVER TO YOU!

One important element of breakdowns, which ties into overlapping action, is the reversal. The term *reversal* is usually mentioned when talking about the spine of the character and how it changes from one pose to the next. If your spine is shaped like a simple C curve, and moves to a reverse Ɔ curve, you've just done a reversal. Reversals are not just limited to the spine, however. They can be in any part of the body, like the overall shape of an arm. Regardless, when creating a breakdown between reversals, we usually see an S curve in that transition. Breaking down a reversal, creating an S curve, can be confusing at first, but if you know what's leading the action and what's following the action, you're already halfway there.

Let's take a look at Mr. Buttons's tail swinging side to side in Figure 4.7. On the extremes, we have subtle C curves and a reversal of the overall shape when you compare the two. Since the base of the tail is leading the action and will arrive first, it should more closely match the curve of the next pose. Conversely, since the tip of the tail is following behind, its curve should more closely match the previous pose, creating the overlapping action. Incorporating overlapping action into our breakdowns is a more advanced workflow for sure, and it can get overwhelming at times. However, by simply deciding what's leading the action, we can then determine what's staying behind and pose our breakdown accordingly.

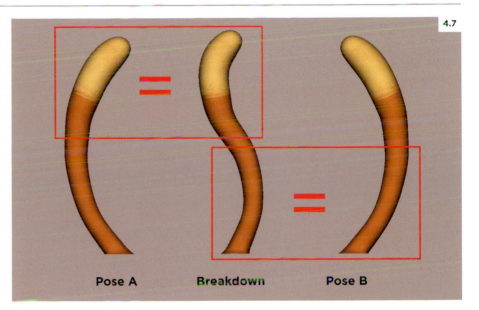

4.7

4.7 S Curve Breakdown
Notice the S curve breakdown when dealing with reversals, where the base of the tail matches the curvature of the next pose, and the tip of the tail matches the curvature of the previous pose.

Pose A   Breakdown   Pose B

Smears, Motion Lines, and Multiples

4.8

4.8 *Hotel Transylvania*, 2012
Motion blur, while not entirely new to CG artists, as seen here in the background of this image from *Hotel Transylvania*, was something old-school traditional animators had to do without. Instead, they employed creative techniques like smears and dry-brush to help bridge the visual gap when they needed to animate a fast-moving object or character.

Smears, motion lines, and multiple limbs—the fun, inventive, cartoony solutions to the problem of motion blur—tend to predominantly occur during the breakdown. However, since their application can be pretty involved, we're going to cover those techniques in more detail in Chapter 6. Also, because they can be time consuming to create, it is sometimes wise to incorporate them during or after the refining phase, as any changes to your shot after you've created these effects can be particularly painful. For now, you can continue to animate your shot without them, knowing that there may be some strobing issues with your animation, where the images appear to stutter on playback, because of the large spacing gaps.

I know that's a lot to ask as they really are a lot of fun to create, and it may be a lot to ask of a director who may want to see some of these effects early on to see how they're going to play out. So feel free to skip ahead to Chapter 6 and experiment with them at this phase of the process, but keep a loose grip on them, knowing that they may be completely changed in the course of finaling your animation.

LIKING WHAT YOU
GET VS GETTING
WHAT YOU LIKE

BUILDING
A BETTER
BREAKDOWN

INTERVIEW:
PEPE SÁNCHEZ

STEP-BY-STEP
WALKTHROUGH

OVER TO YOU!

TIP | BREAKING DOWN BREAKDOWNS

For complex actions, one breakdown is unlikely to be enough. So how do you handle a transition between two extremes that requires more than one breakdown? Regardless of how many breakdowns I need, which may not be entirely clear until I start creating them, I will always start with a breakdown at the midpoint between the two extremes. So if the first extreme is at frame 10 and the next extreme is at frame 18, I'll create my breakdown on frame 14, the halfway point between the two. After I've created this first breakdown, if more breakdowns are needed, I'll then consider that breakdown to be a new extreme and repeat the process, dividing and conquering, so to speak.

By the time I'm done, I may have a keyframe on every second frame. I may even have a keyframe on every frame through a complicated transition—which happens quite frequently. Don't ever feel like you can't have a keyframe on every frame. For cartoony action, this level of control is often necessary. When the keyframes are one frame apart, you may need to shift them around to make room for more breakdowns. This is perfectly fine. I am almost always shifting my timing around when creating breakdowns.

PEPE SÁNCHEZ

Pepe Sánchez is a renaissance man when it comes to animation, having started out as a 2D inbetweener and working his way up to traditional animator. He then transitioned over to computer animation, eventually becoming an animation supervisor on the popular preschool show, *Pocoyo* (2005–2010), and then an animation director on the *Jelly Jamm* (2011–) series. Pepe took some time to talk about his experiences and share his thoughts on animation.

How did you get your start in animation?
I started 35 years ago in traditional animation as an inbetweener, working just from the ground up, trying to learn from the animators around me. Some of the first projects I worked on were one of the *Asterix* movies and *Babar the Elephant* (1989–1991). I was doing that, just as an inbetweener. I think my first animation was Disney's *TaleSpin* (1990–1991) and then one of the Batman TV series. I then moved to Ireland where I was working for Don Bluth's studio for a few years. Don Bluth was leaving for Phoenix, and they were finishing up *The Pebble and the Penguin* (1995) when I first started. I worked on *All Dogs Go to Heaven 2* (1996).

Well, after that, I moved back to Spain, trying to get some work in traditional animation there, but it was the beginning of 3D, so as you know a traditional animator trying to get into 3D animation was not easy. It was difficult. If you're a traditional animator, studios don't think you can do 3D, so to get your first job in 3D was not easy. But I did get my start in 3D, working on a Spanish movie for Dygra Films. After that I started working on *Pocoyo*, as an animator, and within a few months I became a supervisor, working there for six years. I then worked on *Jelly Jamm* as animation director. That was my last big job because I began doing my own show a couple of months ago called *Bugsted* (2013). It's a kind of multimedia project where we have video games, toys, an app for mobile phones, and a TV series with 13 one-minute episodes. It's very funny, more for adults than preschoolers, though. Now I'm doing another TV series, a preschool one with puppets. I like to try many different things. I don't want to stay too long in the same thing. It gets boring, so I usually move around a lot. I'm also trying to get into traditional animation again. I love doing traditional animation, more so than doing 3D.

You had mentioned your struggle getting into 3D because you were seen as just a traditional animator. Now, having successfully transitioned over, has your experience as a traditional animator helped you when it comes to animating in 3D?

Well, I do think we have an advantage as traditional animators because of the way we learned it—it requires more patience because it takes longer to learn. And you have the time to really grasp the concepts, the principles that the 3D people don't necessarily have. They go really fast—going through school in one year and then straight into animation. I think that's not the ideal way to do things, you know? They learn to use the tools, but not really how to animate. This is a question of time. With this profession, it's not something you can learn really fast. You need time. So, for example, silhouette, appealing shapes, arcs—all that, for people that come from a traditional animation background, is easier. Especially when you work as an inbetweener, you really need to know your arcs.

You have also done some character design—how does the design of the character impact the animation?

It impacts it a lot. Take for example some of the characters in *Pocoyo*. Pato, the duck, he's made of different pieces put together and that inspired us animators to do crazy things with him. So he moves in a particular way because of his design, it's the way he's constructed. Elly, for example, the elephant, is softer, so she doesn't move as crazily. And she doesn't move the same as Pocoyo, the main character, so the design and the animation are closely tied together.

You've had your hands in many different aspects of animated filmmaking. You've done supervision, you've done design, you've directed—what has motivated you to wear so many hats?

Even before animation, I was doing comic books, storyboards, layouts, things like that. I moved to animation because I really liked it, but it's not the only thing I wanted to do. I really like telling stories, and you need to learn a little bit of everything if you want to tell a story—color design, character design, environment design—you need to learn all that if you want to be a successful director.

Let's talk a little bit about *Pocoyo* and *Jelly Jamm* because they have a really unique style that I think is rather groundbreaking in terms of computer animation. So can you tell me about how that style developed?

It didn't happen overnight. It was a lot of trial and error. One of the directors, especially for the first season, was Guillermo García Carsí. Before *Pocoyo*, I believe he was working for Cartoon Network, and he's a crazy man, as crazy as Pato, the duck. He gave a lot of input on the series, and had a strong vision for how we should animate it. But the animators all shared their visions as well, so the style developed with the first season, with the input of everybody there, not just the directors. One of the points was to avoid the fluid motion that a lot of 3D has, where you would never hold a drawing, everything has to be moving. For example, in *Pocoyo*, we didn't even spline the animation and we preferred to animate with a dope sheet.

So you didn't even touch the Graph Editor?

No, we didn't touch the Graph Editor. We would check it if something was out of arc or to solve problems, but in general we worked with a dope sheet. Just like traditional animation, we created the main keys and then put everything in linear, nothing in spline. We made the in-betweens ourselves and favored them to one extreme or the other, like in traditional animation, like a third or a half. In doing it this way, we were trying to get away from the computer filling in all the gaps for us.

Did it take a long time for the animators to adapt to that kind of workflow?

Yeah, it took almost a year. Because in 3D animation everyone is used to animating the spline way, the Graph Editor way, so it was tough. We used the short film *The Monk and the Fish* (1994) as inspiration for the kind of spasmodic timing, where there aren't a lot of in-betweens, using the least amount of images as possible. We'd have two extremes, and the slow-in and slow-out would need three drawings each, no more than four. So if you go frame by frame in *Pocoyo*, you will notice all of that. You also see a lot of held poses, where we would keep Pocoyo held for 10 or 20 frames, no problem.

Working that way, you were probably able to get a lot of footage out, right?

A full episode would take almost a month, from animatic to final cut. But in animation, it was a week. We worked in two teams, one working the morning, the other working the afternoons. So we did two episodes every week. Each animator did around 500 frames a week.

Now on *Jelly Jamm*, you were doing multiple limbs, cartoony cheats like that. Did decisions like that come from the director or did the animators have the freedom to try different things?

There was a lot of freedom. At the beginning, the director told us what he wanted, and the references were Chuck Jones, Tex Avery, and *Pocoyo* as well, because it was the beginning of that style in 3D, so we tried to keep a little of the style of *Pocoyo* on *Jelly Jamm*. After that, we experimented with the style to see how far we could take it. We tried motion blur, but it didn't work for us. It was too expensive to get something right with motion blur, so in the end we chose to go with really strong poses, stretching everything and using multiple legs or arms. The rigs had six legs and four arms built into them so you could use them if you needed.

Seeing as you've done some supervision and directing, what do you look for in the animation reels you review?

I want to see something different from the rest. And that's a difficult thing, because now, with some of the online schools, I think they're very good, but the reels are more or less all the same. Same kind of exercises, same rigs to animate, so when I see something that's different, it stands out. If there's something fun there, something that makes me laugh, getting to my emotions—that kind of thing. Of course, I'm always trying to see if the principles are there— balance, weight, acting, as well. My advice will be to at least try not to use the same free rigs everyone else uses. Try to find something unique, something that is your own design, if possible.

Do you have any other advice for students looking to get in the industry?

Yes, do something different besides animation—this is difficult. Seriously, though, just go for it! If it is your dream, you will have to fight and study a lot and try to get there. Try, and try, and try. Keep going, keep going.

STEP-BY-STEP WALKTHROUGH

Exploring the Options

In this walkthrough, I'll be creating a couple of breakdowns, detailing the thought process behind them. The first one will be the breakdown between the anticipation pose I created at the end of Chapter 3 to the following pose, where he's standing at the door to his blind date's house. This same breakdown will also be where I smear the character, which we'll discuss in Chapter 6. While the smearing will be a consideration when constructing this pose, my first priority is to create an appealing breakdown that takes into account what we've already discussed in this chapter.

For this breakdown, I'm going to go back to my planning, as I already made some exploratory sketches as to how Mr. Buttons might transition between these two poses. The smear pose on the lower left corner of Figure 4.9 is what I'll be working toward. In the breakdown, Mr. Buttons will be leading with his left arm and leg, with the right side of his body dragging behind.

4.9 The options

4.9

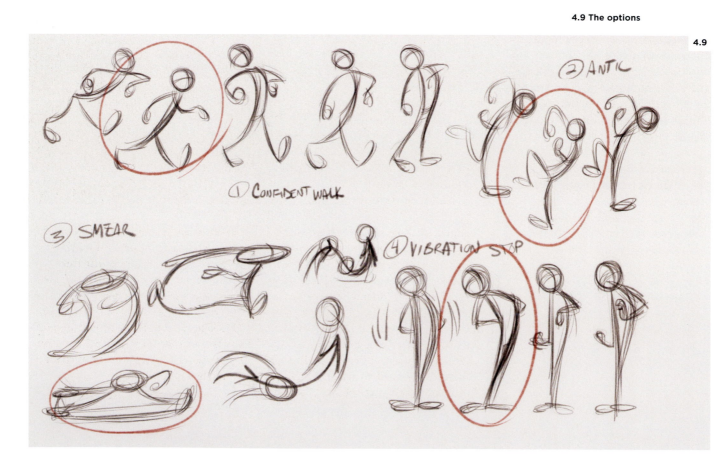

① CONFIDENT WALK

② ANTIC

③ SMEAR

④ VIBRATION STOP

LIKING WHAT YOU
GET VS GETTING
WHAT YOU LIKE

BUILDING
A BETTER
BREAKDOWN

INTERVIEW:
PEPE SÁNCHEZ

**STEP-BY-STEP
WALKTHROUGH**

OVER TO YOU!

4.10

1. For breakdowns, I always use the tweenMachine. Since my breakdown will be at the midpoint between the two poses, I clicked on the middle button in the tweenMachine window. Figure 4.10 shows my first pose, the breakdown the tweenMachine created, and my final pose. The results aren't all that exciting, but it does give me something to work with so I can build the pose from there.

4.11

2. The first thing I focused on was to have Mr. Buttons arc down through this breakdown, dragging his drawers across the floor (see Figure 4.11). Since he's in an upright position on the extremes, this will make for a nice swooping motion that takes into account the force of gravity. I also incorporated some overlapping action by having his left foot extend far forward and his right foot staying behind. His feet are, in essence, spanning the distance between the two poses. This will help bridge the gap and, along with the smear that will be added later, reduce the amount of negative space between the two extremes when he's in motion. This is important in that it will alleviate any possible strobing, since the timing between his starting and ending pose will only be a few frames.

4.12

4.13

3. I wanted to give Mr. Buttons a forward lean through this breakdown, so he'll be rising, head first, into the next pose. This will be cleaner and more direct than having his head drag behind. Even with the forward lean of the body, he was still too tall, so I translated his head down so it's somewhat buried into his chest (see Figure 4.12). His bowtie is barely peeking through, so I'll just hide it completely when I start tweaking the pose. Plus, graphically, that blue bowtie stands out from the sea of orange, so eliminating it will make for a cleaner smear.

4. Just as I sketched out in my planning thumbnail, I've decided to have his arm lead the action of his body (see Figure 4.13). This also ties in nicely with the decision to have him leaning, head first, through this breakdown. In addition, this creates some slight contrast to the move as his entire body is arcing downward, and his hand is moving more or less in a straight line between the two extremes. Lastly, notice the flow that goes through his arms and into his tail, a sweeping curvilinear line that contrasts with the strong horizontal line created by his legs.

LIKING WHAT YOU
GET VS GETTING
WHAT YOU LIKE

BUILDING
A BETTER
BREAKDOWN

INTERVIEW:
PEPE SÁNCHEZ

STEP-BY-STEP
WALKTHROUGH

OVER TO YOU!

5. The breakdown is pretty much done, so now it's time to refine the pose, tweaking his face and using the secondary controls. I've added more drag to his forehead and cheeks and rounded his arms, giving them a more rubber-hose look (see Figure 4.14). I also adjusted his legs so they're flatter along the ground, and added a slight bend to his left foot, showing drag. These changes are subtle but go a long way toward adding appeal. Spacing wise, this pose is spaced evenly between the first pose and the last pose. One breakdown pose will not be enough, so I've decided to have him slow-out of the first pose and snap quickly into the second pose. Since the changes in shape are so drastic between the first pose and this breakdown, we'll be creating another breakdown pose to take control of the outcome, not leaving it up to Maya, our ignorant inbetweener.

4.14

6. Just as I did with my first breakdown, Figure 4.15 was initially built from what the tweenMachine produced, again using the middle button to create a pose that I could build upon. That being said, I did pose the character so that the upper part of his body (hands and head) are heavily favoring the first pose. In fact, I kept the top of his head in the same spot by stretching it out. Page-flipping back and forth (using the comma and period hotkeys) between the first pose and this new breakdown allowed me to translate the top of his head and match it closely. Notice, too, the rubber-hose-like arms and legs. When dealing with fast action, we can break the joints as needed to create fluidity in our motion.

4.15

4.16

7. Even though the last breakdown I created was sufficient for going into spline, I thought I'd add just one more breakdown to really control the motion. In the process of creating it (again using the middle button on the tweenMachine), I thought I'd add in some anticipation by translating his body upward. However, I didn't want his head to move upward, as I thought that might be a bit distracting, so I squashed his head to maintain its position. In the process of doing so, his upper teeth penetrated through his head, and it looked really goofy (see Figure 4.16). Instead of trying to fix it, I decided to make it even more apparent by adjusting his jaw. These are the unplanned happy accidents that occasionally happen; accidents that I absolutely love. It's one of those things that won't be seen by the audience, but if anyone takes the time to frame-by-frame through the animation, they'll get to enjoy it. It's like an Easter egg for animators.

LIKING WHAT YOU
GET VS GETTING
WHAT YOU LIKE

BUILDING
A BETTER
BREAKDOWN

INTERVIEW:
PEPE SÁNCHEZ

STEP-BY-STEP
WALKTHROUGH

OVER TO YOU!

4.17

8. For this next example, I thought I'd choose some extremes to breakdown that are less exaggerated. In this scene, Mr. Buttons has just knocked on the door and is going to pull out some lovely flowers from behind him (see 4.17). I still plan on doing some cartoony stuff but it'll be on a much smaller scale. Like all breakdowns, I again employed the tweenMachine, giving me something to build upon. And again, like most

of the breakdowns I create, I used the middle button on the tweenMachine to give me a halfway point between the two extremes. The breakdown it created is actually pretty decent looking. His head is following a nice arc, but there's no overlapping action, so everything is moving at the same time and the spacing is dead even. Time to make it more interesting.

4.18

9. My workflow should be pretty predictable to you by now, as I first work on the core of the character and go out from there. For this breakdown, I wanted to have his hips lead and have the chest and head follow (see Figure 4.18). While he's not doing a reversal in the curvature of his spine from one extreme to the next, I still wanted to incorporate an S curve that would create the overlapping action I was looking for. Also, not only is his head going to follow a nice arc on the way back, but there's a slight arc on his hips as he dips through the breakdown. And while his body is creating a more complex shape, his tail is being slightly simplified, straightening out from an S shape into a more simple curve, in an effort to show his tail dragging behind the main action. Quite a bit has changed from where I started. I went from even spacing on every part of his body to having his head favor the first extreme and the rotation of his hips favor the next extreme.

LIKING WHAT YOU
GET VS GETTING
WHAT YOU LIKE

BUILDING
A BETTER
BREAKDOWN

INTERVIEW:
PEPE SÁNCHEZ

STEP-BY-STEP
WALKTHROUGH

OVER TO YOU!

4.19

4.20

10. We may not be able to have contrasting arcs in this example, but we do have an opportunity to have contrasting action—where his body is moving one way and his arm is moving in the opposite direction. This unfolding of the character will make for more interesting action, so I'm going to capitalize on it by making it clearer, extending his arm out to create more negative space in the crook of his elbow (see Figure 4.19). Also, Mr. Buttons produces the daisies from nowhere, sometimes referred to as cartoon space. This is a perfect example of a cartoony idea, as opposed to a cartoony motion. As for the daisies, they are simply following the path of action, the arc, created by the arm and wrist.

11. Since his head is rotating forward slightly, I decided to pull back on his forehead to elongate his face and create drag. I also tweaked the shape of the arm, giving it a more curvilinear quality (see Figure 4.20). One thing to note is that the timing of the action will determine how much curve I can add to his arm. If it's a slow action, happening over eight to 12 frames, curving his arm this much will draw attention to itself and make the character feel too loosey-goosey. However, the snappy timing of this move, happening over three to four frames, affords me this opportunity to exaggerate the pose more.

4.21

12. One more breakdown was needed to complete the action, so I used the tweenMachine to create a new breakdown in-between the one I just created and the final pose (see Figure 4.21). To make the move snappier, I didn't use the middle button on the tweenMachine but opted instead to use the second button from the right so it will favor the final pose more. As you can see, it's fairly close to the final pose. It's a serviceable pose and would probably work out okay, but, again, it's just not very interesting, so I need to make some adjustments to it.

LIKING WHAT YOU
GET VS GETTING
WHAT YOU LIKE

BUILDING
A BETTER
BREAKDOWN

INTERVIEW:
PEPE SÁNCHEZ

STEP-BY-STEP
WALKTHROUGH

OVER TO YOU!

4.22

13. Since the S curve of his spine was rather pronounced in the original breakdown, I still wanted there to be some semblance of it through his body and show that it had worked its way toward his head. Also, to avoid having everything slow-in to the final pose, I decided to have his arm overshoot its final resting place (see Figure 4.22). I also thought about the material properties of the daisies and how there'd be quite a bit of wind resistance caused by all the little flower petals, so I have them lagging behind considerably. Actually, that's not quite true. I simply wanted to have more drag on them and needed a justification other than I thought it'd look cool. By now, I hope you can see how even the tiniest modifications to what Maya gives you can make your breakdowns far more interesting and effective.

BREAK IT DOWN!

Breakdowns are a joy to create because, at this point, the main performance is already worked out and you can have a lot of fun thinking about how you're going to transition between your storytelling and extreme poses.

It's time to switch hats from an actor to an inventor, coming up with unique solutions and creative problem solving. Continue working on your shot, breaking down the action, and remember to incorporate:

— slow-in

— slow-out

— overlapping action

— arcs

Also be thinking about where you might want to include some of the fun, cartoony techniques we'll be talking about in Chapter 6.

CHAPTER FIVE
REFINE

Richard Williams, author of *The Animator's Survival Kit*, is a huge advocate of unplugging, admonishing us to cut out the distractions so we can give our work our complete attention. I do agree with this, especially during the planning, pose-test, and breakdown phases. But digging into the Graph Editor to refine our motion is more a technical task than an artistic one, and we are, in some sense, changing hats. The more we're acquainted with the Graph Editor, the more rote our work becomes. At this point, I almost need a distraction so as to help make the time more enjoyable when I'm noodling with the curves, so I'll frequently listen to music or podcasts.

Admittedly, I'm not a huge fan of spending countless hours in the Graph Editor, but I want to be careful not to bias anyone against it. When I first understood the Graph Editor, my eyes were opened to just how powerful a tool it was. In a purely analytical way, the curves in the Graph Editor are the animation! It's all about values (numbers) changing over time. While I will be covering some ways in which you can refine your motion without even touching the curves, it's critical that you have a basic understanding of what the curves do and how to fix things when you get into trouble. One of my goals with this chapter is to give you some practical tips on how you can do just that, but the primary goal is to take your existing roughed-in animation and sand off the jagged edges to make your motion beautiful.

ACHIEVING POLISH

We know what polished animation looks like, but what is the essence of refined motion? How do we achieve it? Polish is primarily two things—arcs and spacing. There's no magical formula, no secret sauce—it really all comes down to arcs and spacing. We've covered both these concepts in the previous chapters but in this part of the animation process, they're the prime focus. Without either one, your animation will have hitches in the motion that can be a distraction for the viewer, so it's important that you spend the time to refine your motion.

Developing your eye to see the arcs and spacing will take time and experience, so knowing when they're off may not be readily obvious. There are some helpful draw-over tools to help you check your arcs and spacing, and I'd highly recommend checking some of these out. You can see the Tip box on page 125 for some suggestions. A secondary focus of polish is making sure you don't have any intersecting geometry, like a foot going through the floor or the fingertips going through a held prop. Those kinds of fixes are straightforward enough so we'll

focus our attention on the polishing aspects concerned with refined motion, arcs, and spacing.

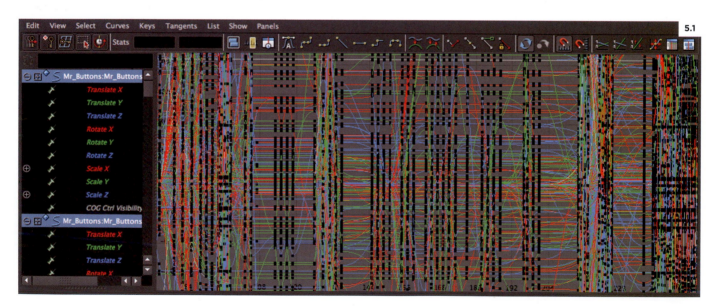

5.1

5.1 The Graph Editor
The Graph Editor (AKA the spaghetti box) is a source of terror for many students. And from looking at all the curves, you can certainly understand why. But fear not, help is on the way!

THE TERRIFYING
TRANSITION   FINAL POLISH

INTERVIEW:
T. DAN HOFSTEDT

STEP-BY-STEP
WALKTHROUGH   OVER TO YOU!

ACHIEVING POLISH

It Takes Time

5.2 *Kung Fu Panda 2*, 2011
While polish is primarily concerned with arcs and spacing, it's also about fixing geometry intersections. Anytime a character touches something, care must be taken to make sure there are no penetration problems. The animator working on this shot had his work cut out for him, making sure none of the bunnies intersected Po.

The one pitfall I've seen over and over again with students is how little time they devote to this part of the animation process. As a general rule, refining your motion typically takes as much time as it does to plan, pose-test, and create breakdowns. When you're at the point where you're ready to refine, you should be at the halfway point in the schedule. Different productions demand different levels of refinement. A feature film will have a much higher demand than, say, commercial or direct-to-video work. The same goes for visual style. If you're working on a production with a more limited-animation style where there are static holds, the refining stage is going to take less time. For our purposes, it's important that you learn to polish at the feature level so you can adapt to any style and schedule. So plan accordingly, and give yourself plenty of time to spline and refine your motion.

THE TERRIFYING TRANSITION

Going Spline

Assuming that we're working with stepped tangents, we first need to convert our curves to another tangent type before we start refining the motion. This can be a very scary moment, where your beautiful, snappy, crisp animation is turned to mush. However, by using the four-frame rule (see Chapter 4) as a guide and by using some of the techniques outlined below, we can mitigate the pain somewhat by allowing us to get back to something more closely resembling what we had in our breakdown pass.

A few Maya releases ago, spline was the tangent type most animators switched into from stepped mode. One of the big pitfalls of spline tangents was overshoot, where the curve would overshoot past the value of the key we set (See Figure 5.3). This created a lot of extra work for us as we had to go in and adjust all those overshoots to get back to something that more closely resembled what we had in stepped. Recent Maya releases have added a new tangent type called *auto tangents*. It's a lot like spline but with one major improvement—no dreaded overshoot. It's not perfect, and it sometimes does some strange things when keys are added later on, but overall, it's a great tangent type to go into from stepped.

That being said, some animators prefer spline tangents *because* of the overshoot, as it can loosen up the motion and create some happy accidents that make the animation look more natural. Some animators prefer linear tangents when going out of stepped. Others prefer going into clamped tangents, where the tangents will automatically flatten if the values between the adjacent keyframes are close or identical. There are even some that stay in stepped and just key each frame where they want to add in more detail. Whatever the tangent type, use whatever works for you. That's one of the great things about computer animation—there are many ways to approach the same problem, so feel free to experiment with something new—or stick with what you know. All that matters is the end result. If you are going from stepped tangents into another tangent type, however, your holds will likely be lost. We'll cover that in the next section.

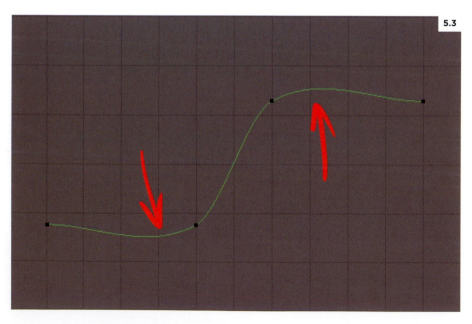

5.3

5.3 Curve overshoot
Here we see an example of curve overshoot, indicative of the spline tangent type where the animation goes beyond the keyframe.

One way to convert all your curves to a different tangent type is to first make sure all the controls are selected on the character rig; then select all the curves in the Graph Editor and just click on the tangent type button of your choice (see Figure 5.4). However, unless you've framed all your keys in the Graph Editor by pressing the A hotkey, you may miss some animation curves and have curves in different tangent types. An easier and quicker way is to double-click in the timeline, selecting all your keyframes, and then right-click anywhere in the selection and choose the tangent type of choice from the pop-up menu. Like the Graph Editor approach, this too has a caveat in that the only animation curves that will be affected by the change will be the ones visible in the Time Slider. So make sure you've got the entirety of your animation visible when using this method. When changing your tangent type, it's also important to change the tangent type in the preferences. You can get to your preference panel here: Window > Settings > Preferences > Preferences (see Figure 5.5). This ensures that any newly created keys are going to match the tangent type you just converted your animation curves into.

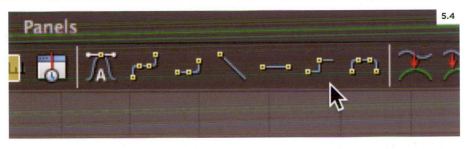

5.4 Accessing tangent types
At the top of the Graph Editor window we have quick access to Maya's different tangent types.

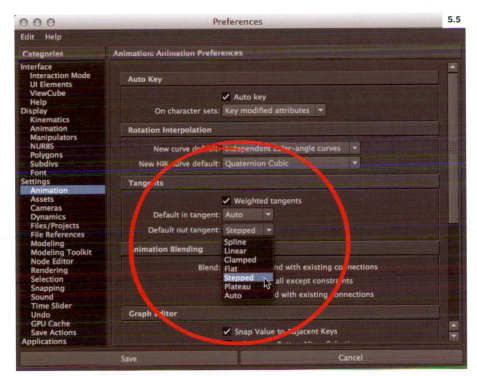

5.5 Tangent type preferences
The selection of tangent types in the preferences allows you to set the tangent type for newly created keys. It's important to note that this has no effect on existing animation.

Moving Holds

The first thing you'll notice when moving out of stepped tangents is that all your holds are gone. That 12-frame hold is now a soupy slough and has lost any trace of crispness. Right after going into spline, I tie down my holds. How do I do this? I start by copying and pasting the pose where the hold begins to where it should end, which is usually two to four frames before the next keyframe. In doing so, I just created a copied pair, and if I'm using auto-tangents, it will create a static hold.

If you're not going for a static-hold look, how do you convert a static hold into a moving hold, where there's some slight movement to help keep the character alive? This is where the tweenMachine comes in. Not only is the tweenMachine, great at creating breakdowns, it's also pretty handy for moving holds. In the timeline, go to the first frame of your hold, bring up the tweenMachine and with everything selected, click on the rightmost button (see Figure 5.6). This will convert your first keyframe to be 75 percent of the following keyframe. Math aside, it's basically converting this pose to be a combination of the previous and next poses but strongly favoring the next one so that it's creating a nice slow-in. Again, you may have to reapply auto-tangent to take care of any wonky curve behavior.

This is one of those tricks that quickly creates moving holds and is great for getting us most of the way there. However, as you can imagine, applying

this to all your holds is going to create a bit of repetition in the way your moving holds settle—it's sort of an assembly line approach to your moving holds. To keep things natural feeling and to add some contrast, you'll need to revisit these holds, adding little nuances to the motion to liven things up a bit. You can overlap some of the parts of the character at the beginning of this hold to help break it up—like dragging an arm or head behind. Or you can have some parts of the body overshoot and settle back—these are the same concepts you applied to your breakdowns, just at a smaller level. You can also break up a moving hold by adding in subtle bits of animation business. For instance, I use headshakes to a fault and that's just one way you can break up a moving hold. Blinks, eye-darts, subtle weight-shifts, and breathing are just a few more. Since these additions will likely break up the cleanness of your poses by moving away from having every part of the character keyed on the same frame, I tend to layer these in after I've done a broad retiming pass. We'll cover that next.

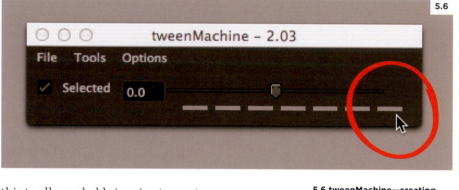

5.6

5.6 tweenMachine—creating a moving hold
On the tweenMachine, aside from the middle button, which is the one I use to create most of my breakdowns, my next favorite is the rightmost button, as it gives me a great starting point to create a moving hold.

Retime

5.7

When you convert your tangents from stepped to any other tangent type, the timing changes. Whereas in stepped, your keyed pose will not be displayed until the timeline has arrived at that frame, in spline, your character starts working his or her way into the pose before that keyframe. Even if you've set many keys to try to make the transition into spline less painful, inevitably, some retiming will be necessary to get it back to the timing of how things looked in stepped.

After you've keyed in your holds, take some time to shift your keyframes around. I have used the dope sheet or the Graph Editor to do this, but that was before I knew I could easily retime my animation in the Time Slider. After you've selected all the character controls, holding down shift while clicking on a keyframe in the timeline selects it, and you can then drag it left or right to change its position. You can also shift-drag a selection of frames, and using the little arrow handles in the middle, you

can shift that entire section around (see Figure 5.7). By grabbing the arrows on the ends of the selection, you can scale those keyframes to condense or expand the timing. Keep in mind that when doing this your keyframes are going to end up on noninteger frame numbers, and you'll want to fix that afterwards.

With the keyframes still selected, right-click anywhere in the selection, and choose Snap from the pop-up menu (see Figure 5.8). If you've got keys on every frame of a section, occasionally you'll get an error saying that Maya had to skip snapping on some of the keys. Maya simply doesn't know where to snap them

since there are too many keys for the available frames. In those cases, you'll have to rearrange them manually—perhaps even deleting some keys to make them all fall on integer frames. Snapping keys does change the timing a bit so anytime you do this, you'll want to fix any timing issues. You can also use the double-click method of selecting everything in the Time Slider, which can be a little timesaver if you need to make broad adjustments to your keyframes.

At this point, assuming you've created enough breakdowns and tied down your holds, your animation should be looking fairly close to what you had in stepped mode—which is great! The transition is complete and the meltdown/panic attack phase is over. Plus all your keys are still nicely organized with every part of the character keyed on the same frames! Why is that important? This makes broad changes fairly easy to implement if you get any major notes from the supervisor or director this late in the game.

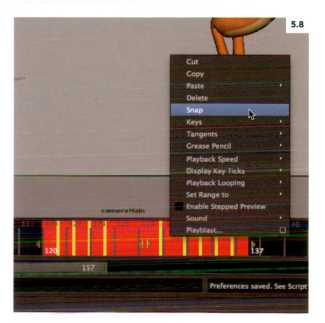

5.8

5.7 Time Slider
Highlighting a frame or selection of frames in the timeline allows you to easily manipulate its position in the Time Slider.

5.8 Snap keyframes
Make sure you snap keyframes after scaling them in the timeline, so they snap to the nearest frame number.

FINAL POLISH

Now you're ready to sand off the rough edges and fully refine your animation. There are two primary ways to refine your motion. You can go the Graph Editor route, or simply add keys to define your arcs and spacing in the camera view. Both have their pros and cons, and we'll cover them in a little more detail next.

Polishing with the Graph Editor

Polishing in the Graph Editor seems like a daunting task. Even if you're comfortable with the Graph Editor, there can be thousands of individual animation channels, so the prospect of going through each can be overwhelming. The good news is that not every curve needs to be touched. All that matters is what it looks like in the camera view. If there are some ugly, jagged curves in the Graph Editor, but the animation looks great in the camera view, then why waste the time making pretty curves? The same goes for unnecessary keys. I once had an instructor who wanted the students to remove any keys that weren't doing anything, like when you come across a bunch of keys on a flat curve. That seems like a colossal waste of time to me. The adage, if it ain't broke, don't fix it, applies here. However, for those who prefer working with a cleaner looking editor, Maya has a useful shortcut for deleting all the keyframe data on a channel if there's no animation on it. You can access the command through Edit > Delete All by Type > Static Channels.

What I typically recommend is to start with the core of the character and work your way out, polishing as you go. We know that most motion originates from the hips so it makes good sense to start there when refining your animation. You can then break it down by each individual channel, working through each one, looking for any unusual hiccups in the curve, adjusting to refine the motion. Generally speaking, the curves of the main body control should be fairly pretty looking. Unless there's some reason for an abrupt change in direction (like a character hitting a wall), the curves should have a nice flow. As you get further from the core of the character, you'll start to see more interruptions in the flow of the curve. This is to be expected because of the parent-child relationship of the controls—the children inherit the motion of the parents, and this will inevitably lead to jagged curves.

ACHIEVING POLISH   THE TERRIFYING TRANSITION

FINAL POLISH

INTERVIEW: T. DAN HOFSTEDT   STEP-BY-STEP WALKTHROUGH   OVER TO YOU!

When working through an animation channel, you may not immediately know what this curve does. In those cases, I'll typically grab the curve and move it up and down, changing the value, and seeing the results in the camera view. Then, armed with that knowledge, I can safely proceed to polish. Don't be afraid of the Graph Editor. Sure, it's the source of all the power in the animation universe, but trepidation is not how you're going to tame this intimidating beast. Be ruthless in your pursuit of Graph Editor mastery. As you work your way through the curves, experiment. See what happens when you change the value. See what happens when you offset the timing of the keys on the curve. Many times, you'll be pleasantly surprised by the results, and your animation will be all the better because of it.

One other benefit of the Graph Editor is that when you encounter gimbal lock (where you get crazy rotations between keys), there's a magical option within reach. It's called the Euler Filter, and it can be found in the Curves menu in the Graph Editor. It may look as though it should be pronounced like "ruler," without the "r"—but it's actually pronounced like "oiler." Regardless of how you pronounce it, clicking on this option can fix those rotations automatically. It only seems to work

about 50 percent of the time. But when it does work, it's absolutely magical. So how do you fix gimbal lock when the Euler Filter fails? Sometimes, deleting the errant key and reposing the control will work. When that fails, you may just have to key every frame through that transition. It's a bit of a pain to work that way, but there are rare occasions when that's the best option.

5.9 *Horton Hears a Who!*, **2008**
One of the hallmarks of feature animation is the level of quality. A large part of that comes down to that last 10 percent, where all the rough edges in the animation have been sanded smooth. Blue Sky Studios spends a great deal of time in the polishing phase, as can be evidenced by their beautifully expressive animation in films like *Horton Hears a Who!*

Polishing without the Graph Editor

In my career as an animator, I've come across a small number of fellow animators who never touch the Graph Editor. The first one I met was Ken Duncan (Interviewed in Chapter 1), and I was completely perplexed at how this was possible. This was long before I adopted my current workflow and most of my time was spent in the Graph Editor as a result. It's not that Ken doesn't know how to work in the Graph Editor, it's just that he chooses not to use it, only looking at the curves if there's a gimbal lock problem. Ken, and those like him, are a rare breed, but the more I animate, the less time I find myself spending in the Graph Editor as well. And there have been a number of shots I've worked on where I haven't touched it at all. I find that the cartoony style of animation, where you're more likely to sculpt each frame, is more conducive to that way of working. For most shots, I find myself using a combination of both. I'll typically start out in the curves, working on the core of the character, and then as I work out toward the extremities, I find it's

just easier and more direct to get the polish I want by directly manipulating those parts in the camera view, adding in keyframes as needed. It's certainly not for everyone, but, again, that's the beauty of computer animation—there are so many different workflows to choose from.

So how exactly do you polish your animation without using the Graph Editor? Similar to the polishing in the Graph Editor, I'll be looking at my animation through the main camera view and start with the body control, looking at my arcs and spacing and adding keyframes where necessary to control it. If there's a four-frame gap between two poses and the arc is off, I'll typically go to the middle point between those poses and move the control until it's spot on. I'll either scrub through the timeline or, better yet, use the page flipping technique to check for the arc. At that point, there's only a one-frame gap before and after that keyframe and quite often the arcs are fine between those. However, it's

fairly common to key every frame to really take control over the animation. It may seem like an extremely daunting and time-consuming endeavor, but in reality, by having one hand on the page-flipping hotkeys and another hand gently nudging the controller into its proper place, the process can go rather quickly. If you want to do some frame-by-frame level page-flipping instead of just flipping back and forth through the keyframes, you can press the Alt modifier key when using the comma and period keys. And like the Graph Editor polishing approach, once I'm done with the main body action, I can then move outward from there, polishing as I go.

The one caveat to this process, and frankly polishing in general, is that you need to have a well-developed eye to see when the arcs and spacing are off. But there are tools out there to help until that time (see Tip box).

TIP | DRAW-OVER TOOLS

Developing your eye to see your arcs and spacing takes time and practice. Until then, there are some great tools you can use to draw on your screen to help with this. These tools differ from other Maya-specific scripts that allow you to track your arcs on any given object—which are great and useful in and of themselves. The reason I'm not covering them here is that I'm just a huge proponent of making our work on the computer as close to traditional methods as possible. The tools below are more general-purpose ones that primarily do one thing—give you the ability to draw on your screen on top of your work. It's akin to physically drawing on your monitor, which is what we early CG artists used to do. Back in the CRT monitor days, the screen had a glass surface, so it was ideal for using dry-erase markers. Many of today's LCD monitors have a more porous surface, so I don't recommend going that route. Although you could tape a sheet of clear acetate on your LCD screen and go at it with the old-school method.

This is by no means a complete and comprehensive list—just some of the more popular ones that I've used or that other artists have suggested. Some are free, some are not, but even the ones that are not free are relatively inexpensive.

Annotate Pro (PC, $) http://annotatepro.com

Deskscribble (Mac, $) Mac App Store

Epic Pen (PC, Free) http://sourceforge.net/projects/epicpen/

Highlight (Mac, $) Mac App Store

Ink2Go (PC and Mac, Free) http://ink2go.org

Sketch It (PC, Free) http://download.cnet.com/Sketch-It/3000-2072_4-10907817.html

Zoomit (PC, Free) http://technet.microsoft.com/en-us/sysinternals/bb897434.aspx

It's also worth pointing out that Maya version 2014 introduced a built-in Grease Pencil, which offers the same functionality as these draw-over tools with the ability to keyframe the drawings so they can be animated. In the viewport where you want to draw, go to View > Camera Tools > Grease Pencil.

T. DAN HOFSTEDT

T. Dan Hofstedt's resume reads like a who's who in animation. He's worked as a storyboard artist, 2D animator, 3D animator, animation instructor, supervisor, and director. T-Dan's also a gifted musician and has made a couple of albums that showcase his skills as a slack-key guitarist. I had the pleasure of working under his supervision on a couple of the new Looney Tunes CG short films, so I asked if he'd be willing to be interviewed for this book. He politely obliged.

Can you tell me a little about your background in animation and the transition from traditional animation into computer animation?
I attended CalArts in the early eighties learning hand-drawn animation in the Disney style. That led me to work at Hanna-Barbera on the *Smurfs* TV show (1981–1989), then at Sullivan-Bluth for seven years for *American Tail* (1986), *Land Before Time* (1988), *All Dogs Go to Heaven* (1989), *Rock-a-Doodle* (1991), and *A Troll in Central Park* (1994) learning under John Pomeroy and Don Bluth. I started at Disney at the beginning of *Aladdin* (1992) where I stayed for 12 years and eight features.

During the making of *Treasure Planet* (2002), I was assigned to do some exploratory 2D dialog tests for the 3D robot character "B.E.N." They weren't happy with the design of the mouth yet in the early CG models so I was enlisted to try different possible ways he could talk in hand-drawn animation. Working closely with CG lead animator Oskar Urretabizkaia on the character, I was impressed at how much personality he could get out of his CG performances. He really made it look easy. I really wanted to learn to do that. I took some intro to Maya classes at the studio and that began my CG career. I asked if I could be assigned to help animate B.E.N. when animation started. They had already assigned me as lead animator on the

Mister Arrow character (the first mate on the ship, a massive rock creature voiced by Roscoe Lee Browne), and besides, the directors told me that it would be several months before B.E.N. would be ready for animation, as they still had not cast the voice yet and all the final design and rigging still needed to be done.

So I worked on the Arrow character, having lots of fun doing 95 percent of his scenes myself. But after his footage was complete, the rest of the movie still had a lot of footage left to do. I asked if I could be added to the B.E.N. unit. At the time I asked, all the remaining shots had already been cast to the few B.E.N. animators they already had, so there wasn't enough footage to go around for me. Sorry. Oh well. So I helped on some John Silver scenes under Glen Keane plus a few other miscellaneous character shots to help finish the movie. Then we had a screening of the film and one of the notes was that we needed more humor sprinkled in. By this time Martin Short had been cast as the voice of B.E.N. so there were lots of potential for more comedy from that character. Suddenly there were a lot more scenes with B.E.N. than there were before with not much time left to do them. The directors called me in and asked me if I was still interested in animating on B.E.N., and, of course, I jumped at the chance. I ended up doing four shots of B.E.N. which made it into the film.

Naturally there was a learning curve, but when I tried to think of the computer as just a very expensive pencil, it started to get easier. The hard part of animation is really deciding what to do when it comes to acting, timing, and personality. I already had a handle on that, so I just tried to transfer that knowledge to and through the computer.

You have a deep love for music and are quite adept at slack-key guitar. Do you feel your appreciation for music and your skills as a musician have had a meaningful impact on your work as an animator?
There are many parallels between music and animation. Beats, rhythm, phrasing, accents, pacing . . . the list goes on. I think of my animation shots in musical terms, even when there's neither music nor dialog in the shot. Having another creative outlet like guitar helps me expand my experiences to give me appreciation of things other than just animation. No matter what you enjoy doing, whether it be music, sports, the outdoors, gardening, or whatever, your observations of those aspects of your life will inevitably make their way into your work. You are a product of your experiences and observations.

Stylistically, you've gone from one extreme to another from the motion-capture aesthetic of *Monster House* (2006) to the broad cartoony style of Looney Tunes. What kind of preparation is needed when animating outside of a standard animation style?
Animation is such a collaborative medium. By the time animation production is ready to proceed, many creative people have preceded you in the process. Designers, directors, writers, story artists, visual development artists, sculptors, and other animators help shape the early stages of the film. The variety of styles in animation is what can be so cool about it. There are certain rules in the particular universe that's been created where these characters live and breathe. It's great to have limitations to work within, so that you as an artist can get a feel for how your characters must behave in their world.

As for preparation for that as an animator, doing your own homework and research is essential. Reading the script, looking at the boards and designs, asking questions, researching ways characters move (both human and animals). For an established set of classic characters like the Looney Tunes, part of that preparation is to research the great classic films of the past with Bugs,

Observe life, always seek learning, say please and thank you, brush your teeth, wear deodorant, show up to work on time, play nice, and bring something to the table.
T. DAN HOFSTEDT

Daffy, Road Runner, Elmer, and the rest so that you are being consistent with those personalities that everyone in the world has come to instantly recognize. Know who they are and how they would behave in a given situation, and your choices become clearer. The same is true if you are asked to work in a style that is unique like what we did in *Monster House*. Even though the rest of the world had never seen or met these new characters, as an animator you must know the characters so well that when you have creative choices to make, they will be consistent throughout the film. This consistency will help reveal the character to the audience and will hopefully give them a chance to connect with them and care about them.

Could you describe what it was like animating and supervising on some of the Looney Tunes CG short films, which were pushed stylistically to match the aesthetic of the traditional animated shorts?
It was such a thrill and an honor to be involved in those Looney Tunes CG shorts at ReelFX. So many great artists were involved in developing those. The modeling team, the rigging team, the fur and the feathering, and, of course, the animators. They all had a passion for the characters.

We were all paddling in the same direction trying to do our best to make something fun and memorable. It made my job easier. I felt like we were kind of entrusted with a national treasure of sorts. We were the stewards of these classic characters who are known and beloved throughout the world. We knew that we would be scrutinized closely by the audience and our peers, so we wanted to go the extra mile and make it as good as possible. We also knew that there are always so-called purists who would be against the very thought of even attempting to do these classic 2D characters in 3D to begin with. We knew there'd be criticism, but we felt that if we aimed to stay true to the spirit of what made those 2D shorts so wonderful to begin with, we'd have a good chance of being successful.

We were always trying to balance being faithful to the classic style with pushing the boundaries of the stereoscopic format. I'm very proud of what our team was able to do there, but I am most proud that one of my animation heroes, the one and only Eric Goldberg (animator of A*laddin*'s Genie and animation director of *Looney Tunes: Back in Action*) told me we did a good job. That's more praise than I could ever hope to receive, so I guess we done good. . . .

The Looney Tunes shorts made use of some of the more extreme cartoony techniques like multiple limbs, dry-brush, and smears. How did you decide when to incorporate those techniques, or was that largely director driven? Also, since those approaches are primarily addressing the issue of motion blur (or lack thereof), how do you go about deciding which technique to use?
Having had the chance to do 2D animation on *Looney Tunes: Back in Action* (2003) under Eric Goldberg, I was acquainted with using multiple limbs and "smear" drawings for the big screen. This 2D technique grew out of more than just a stylistic choice. It was a hand-drawn way to emulate streaking and motion blur that would happen in live action when there was fast action moving across the screen. The shutter of the live action movie camera was not fast enough to prevent this, so distortions, smears, and multiples in hand-drawn animation grew out of trying to visually connect the shapes as they moved quickly on screen. People got to be very inventive with this and had fun with it (I even did a multiple in *The Lion King* in a shot of Simba!).

Chuck Jones was a master at getting his animators to employ this method. He described animation

as a "flurry of drawings," and what better way to show that than to have a flurry of arms, legs, and eyes indicating fast action? The need of the shot would dictate when and how to use the technique. It should be felt rather than seen. What I mean by that is we shouldn't be calling attention to the fact that, "Hey everybody! Daffy has eight legs!" We should simply get the feeling that Daffy is moving so fast that the camera couldn't keep up with him. We are limited to 24 frames a second, but multiples, blurs, and smears help give us a faster shutter. Rules are made to be broken, but as a general rule I liked to connect the shapes so that the movement of the flurries flowed visually, making it easier on the viewers' eyes.

You've also worked a lot with students, having taught at several art and animation schools. What words of advice do you have for students looking to get their foot in the animation door?
The number one thing to remember is to draw, draw, draw. Wait, that's three things. Well, you get the idea. Even in today's computer-centric world, drawing is an extremely valuable skill. Beyond that, observe life, always seek learning, say please and thank you, brush your teeth, wear deodorant, show up to work on time, play nice, and bring something to the table.

5.10 *Monster House*, **2006**
In terms of exaggerated animation, *Monster House* is on the opposite end of the spectrum from Looney Tunes. However, that doesn't mean the characters can't be expressive in their own right, as seen here in this still from the movie.

STEP-BY-STEP WALKTHROUGH   ### Stepped Tangents

In this walkthrough, I'll be demonstrating many of the techniques discussed in this chapter, as well as problem areas I'm sure will crop up and how to fix them.

1. If you're using stepped tangents, it's good practice to double check and key everything before going into spline. That way, you can be sure that the poses you see in stepped will be the poses you see in spline. As seen in Figure 5.11, I made the mistake of not keying everything on this pose, so there's a good chance I'll get some unexpected results when changing the tangent type. To ensure all your poses are keyed on every control, simply alternate between the S key and the period key to quickly go through your whole animation and lock all your poses down.

2. After selecting all the controls and converting everything to auto tangents, I was expecting to see that my timing was off—that's to be expected. However, I wasn't expecting to see some gimbal lock issues creep up on me like this (see Figure 5.12). When Mr. Buttons went from knocking on the door to pulling the flowers from behind his back, his arm completely rotated the other way, arcing upward, behind his body instead of arcing downward. To make matters worse, the Euler Filter didn't fix this. After looking in the Graph Editor, I noticed the X and Z rotation curves of his shoulder control were shooting off in opposite directions, going into high rotational values. This is one way you can spot gimbal lock within your Graph Editor.

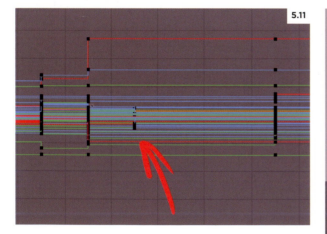

5.11

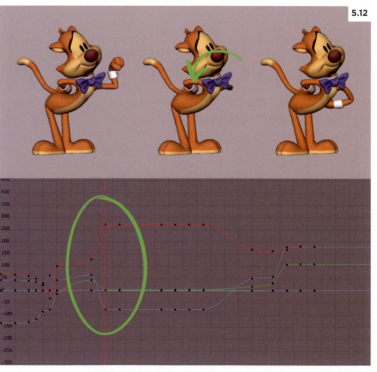

5.12

3. Since the problem seemed to be inherent in the pose itself, I decided to reset the control, zeroing out the rotational values and then rotating the arm back into position. Sure enough, this fixed the problem! You can see the changes in the Graph Editor from before to after in Figure 5.13. I may not always be so lucky. If that hadn't worked, my only course of action would have been to try to brute-force the arm to move in the direction I wanted it to by keying every frame through the transition.

4. There are several places where the timing is off and I need to add some moving holds. Since I address this in essentially the same way in each instance, I'll just detail my process for one area. In this part of the animation, Mr. Buttons has hit a pose on frame 207 where he's presenting the daisies (see Figure 5.14). When this was in stepped mode, he held this pose until the following pose on frame 220. The timing was right and the pose read. Now that it's in spline (Auto Tangents), he still hits the pose on frame 207 but immediately starts to slowly drift into the next pose. This doesn't give the audience time to read this storytelling pose, and it also eliminates the crisp timing that was there when it was in stepped. It's time to create a moving hold.

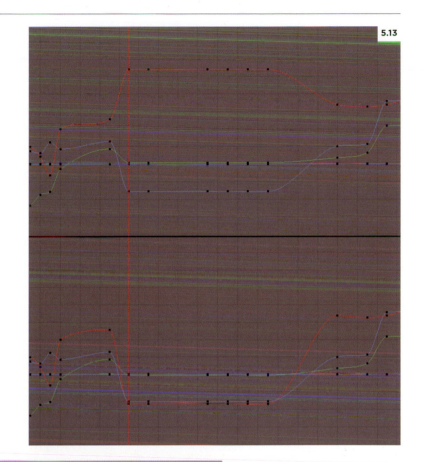

5.13

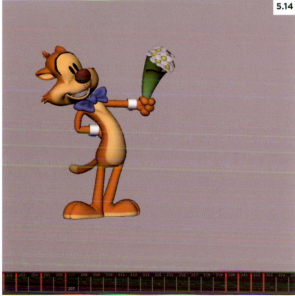

5.14

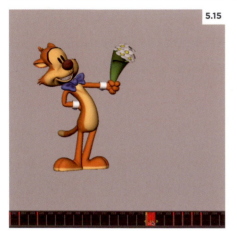

5.15

6. The next step is to return to frame 207, where the pose used to be and using the tweenMachine, again with everything on the character selected, click the rightmost button. This will create a pose that's 75 percent of the final pose on frame 217, giving us a nice slow-in, a moving hold (see Figure 5.16). If you don't want everything moving at the same speed and direction into the final pose on frame 217, now is where you'll want to adjust things, maybe adding more drag to a limb or adding in some

overshoot before settling into the pose on 217. For this pose, I'm going to keep it as-is since my breakdowns included quite a bit of drag and overlap. Plus I want to keep things pretty crisp and tight, without a lot of unnecessary movement during this hold. Lastly, it should be noted that when creating new keyframes, the tangent settings in the preferences will determine the tangent types used. So make sure you change this to the tangent type you're using for your refined animation before moving forward.

5. The first thing I'll do is move the pose that was on frame 207 to frame 217, which is 10 frames later (see Figure 5.15). This will fix the slow drift into the following pose on frame 220 and allow his daisy-presenting pose to be the one that's going to be held. I do this by selecting everything on the character, then shift left-mouse-button clicking on frame 207 in the timeline, and finally middle-mouse-button dragging it to frame 217. Why settle on frame 217? This gives plenty of time for the pose to be read (you need a minimum of six frames for a pose to read), and it also gives us a three-frame transition into the next pose on 220. I also want to keep in mind that I'm not locked down timing-wise on anything, so if I need more or fewer frames for the hold, or more or fewer frames for the transition into the next keyframe, I can shift those things around as needed.

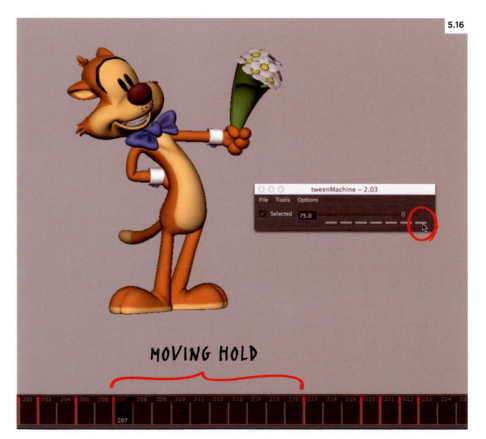

5.16

MOVING HOLD

7. After retiming some of the animation and adding in the moving holds, the animation is looking pretty decent. Now it's time to start refining the motion. Most of my animation polish will be done without using the Graph Editor, working on a frame-by-frame level, moving the controls in the camera view to tie down any parts of the character where the spacing or arcs are off. However, for the walk cycle at the beginning of the shot, I thought I'd try to see what would happen if I started playing around with the curves (see Figure 5.17). Starting with the translate Y of the main body control, I offset the keyframes forward and backward in time by a frame or two. By moving the curves to the left, his up and down movement happens sooner. By moving the curves to the right, his up and down movement happens later. After experimenting with this for a while, I decided that having his up and down movement happen later by a single frame looks really nice. It seems to add just a bit more bounce to the walk—even though the height of his walk hasn't changed. Experimentation like this can go a long way toward refining and plussing the animation.

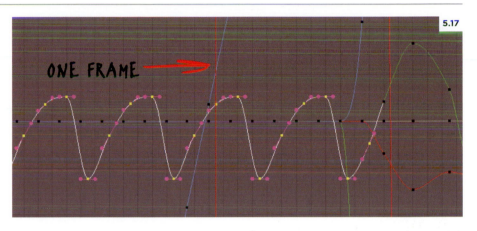

ONE FRAME

5.17

8. In looking at these curves, you might be tempted to go through and clean these up a bit. Every single one of these curves is fairly rough looking (see Figure 5.18). Resist the urge! Pretty curves do not necessarily mean that you have pretty animation. Keep in mind that all that matters is what's seen on screen. These rotational channels are from Mr. Buttons's shoulder during the section of the animation where he goes from being upright into a compressed anticipation. The motion looks fluid through the main camera. If I were to go through and clean up these curves, the change would be a destructive one.

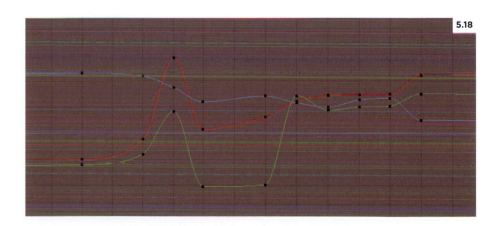

5.18

5.19

9. As I mentioned earlier, I'll be polishing most of this particular animation without the aid of the Graph Editor. I recognize that this may not be the best approach for every animation. However, in this case, because the action is highly caricatured and, as such, has required a large number of breakdowns, polishing without the Graph Editor is probably the best approach. To illustrate this, I've chosen the section of the animation where Mr. Buttons goes from his initial walk into an anticipation pose. Figure 5.19 shows all the breakdowns I created for this transition. Timing-wise, there are roughly two to three frames between each breakdown. Overall, the in-betweens Maya has produced are pretty good. But there are still some places where the spacing and arcs could use some help. We'll look at those next.

10. As we've discussed, wrists are one of the key parts of the character you'll want to track for your arcs and spacing. Figure 5.20 shows the path of action the wrist takes through the transition into his anticipation pose. For the most part, the arcs and spacing look good. However, there are a couple of places, circled in red, where the arcs and spacing could use some fine-tuning. The first circled area represents a spacing problem, where the spacing should be tighter near the change in direction. The second circled area is an arc problem, as I want the arm to swing down before it rises to its resting position. In this case, it just makes more sense to fix this without noodling around with the curves in the Graph Editor, as I can quickly repose the arms on those two trouble spots and be done with it.

11. Figure 5.21 illustrates the revised path of action for the wrist, and it's looking much better. However, now that the main problems have been addressed, I'm noticing that the slow-out and slow-in of the wrist are a bit even, so I'll hit those next before moving on to the next part of the character. And again, I'll use the same process by simply tweaking the arm in the camera view rather than trying to fix this in the Graph Editor. And just to reiterate, give this method a go, but if it doesn't work for you, feel free to return to the Graph Editor. Whatever tool gets the job done is the best tool.

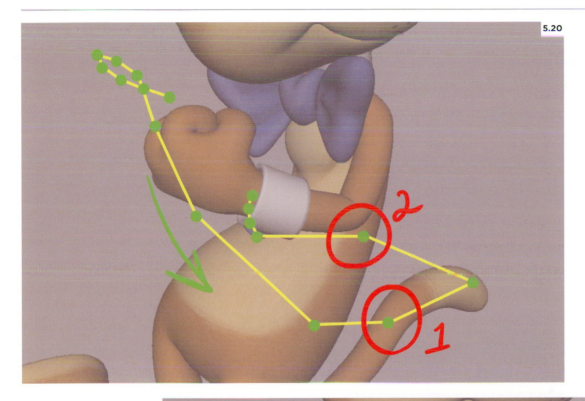

5.20

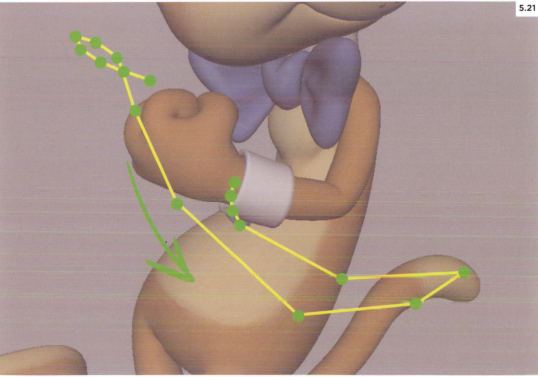

5.21

Just as we switched hats from actor to inventor in the breakdown stage, we've now switched hats from inventor to technician—problem solving and refining our motion and giving it that last 10 percent that makes it shine.

This tends to be the most frustrating part of the process for many students—especially if you're not overly comfortable in the Graph Editor. Familiarity often does breed contempt, but in the case of the Graph Editor, it's the only way to get good at it. It may be overwhelming at first but by taking it control by control and curve by curve, you'll be able to tame this wild beast.

You might be tempted to move on to the fun stuff in the next chapter, but don't skip this very important step. Begin refining the animation on Mr. Buttons, be patient with yourself, and dive in fearlessly!

CHAPTER SIX
CARTOONY
TECHNIQUES

In this final chapter, we'll be covering a handful of some of the crazy cartoony techniques that animators before us have pioneered. I must warn you in advance, however; as if the animation process isn't painstaking enough, incorporating these techniques will put your patience to the test. Every frame matters, but not every frame is created equal. When you're having to pose a half dozen arms and legs, spending countless hours on a single frame of film, that will flash past the audience at 1/24th of a second, you may begin to question your sanity. But anything worth doing is seldom easy, and once the pain of the process has passed and your health and sanity have recovered, you're left with the results of something worthy of frame-by-frame viewing. Let's get started!

THE PROBLEM OF MOTION BLUR

It's important to note that, with the exception of staggers, the following techniques arose in response to the problem of reproducing motion blur. In live-action "motion blur," the smudged distortion of the image when there's fast movement came for free. It is a by-product of how images are captured in the photographic process. Even though blurriness may be undesirable as a static image, when it comes to motion, it's a desirable effect that makes the action more fluid.

To recreate this effect in traditional animation, animators needed to find ways to create the effect of motion blur when animating a fast action. Multiple limbs, motion lines, and smears are all unique approaches to solving this problem, and we'll be covering each one in detail and look at ways in which you can incorporate them into your work. It's also important to note that the problem of motion blur has been solved for many years in computer animation. It can be turned on with the click of

a button, and our renders will start spitting out blurred images without any more work from us. However, when dealing with cartoony action and the use of these techniques, motion blur should be minimally used, if at all, when you're ready to render out your final images, as it will rob your animation of some of its crisp, snappy feel.

THE PROBLEM OF
MOTION BLUR

MULTIPLE LIMBS   MOTION LINES AND   SMEARS   STAGGERS   INTERVIEW: STEP-BY-STEP   OVER TO YOU!
                  DRY-BRUSH   JASON GIGLIOZZI   WALKTHROUGH

6.1

6.1 *Madagascar*, **2005**
Motion blur was used minimally
throughout *Madagascar*.
Instead, the animators made
use of smear frames to cover
large spacing gaps and reduce
strobing.

MULTIPLE LIMBS

One clever solution to the motion blur problem is having multiple instances of a body part helping to bridge a large spacing gap. Since the arms and legs are the most active parts of a character, they're the ones we usually see multiplied when this effect is used. However, any part of the character is game—even the entire body of the character can be given this treatment. So how many multiples should be used? There's no hard and fast rule, but it typically doesn't exceed more than three or four instances of a particular body part. Sometimes, one is enough, but it usually falls into the two to three range. The number of multiples is also dependent on the amount of space that needs to be covered—if the gap is very large, you'll need more limbs to cover

that distance. How far apart they are is also an important consideration, though you'll generally want them to be somewhat evenly spaced. If there is any variation, you might want to have the distance increase with each successive limb. Similarly, if the rig allows, you should adjust the transparency so that the limb that's closest to the main one will be the most opaque and the one that's furthest out will be the most transparent.

Trailing limbs is what usually comes to mind when we think about multiples. However, multiples can also be used anytime you want to create frantic and chaotic movement. A good example of this is when the Road Runner approaches a little pile of birdseed,

strategically placed by his nemesis, Wile E. Coyote. When the Road Runner eats the seed, it's such frenzied action that the best way to represent this is by using multiple instances of his head. I was privileged with animating the first scene of the Road Runner in the short *Coyote Falls* (2010), and, sure enough, it was a birdseed-pecking scene. I ended up using several heads to get the effect, varying the position, expression, and number of heads on each frame. In those instances, the process of creating the effect is a little less systematic than the trailing limbs, so some experimentation will be needed to determine if the effect is working or not. It took me several passes to get the Road Runner's pecking action looking right.

THE PROBLEM OF
MOTION BLUR

MULTIPLE LIMBS

MOTION LINES AND
DRY-BRUSH

SMEARS

STAGGERS

INTERVIEW:
JASON GIGLIOZZI

STEP-BY-STEP
WALKTHROUGH

OVER TO YOU!

6.2 Multiple trailing limbs

Here we see an example of multiple trailing limbs, where each successive arm is spaced further apart and is more transparent.

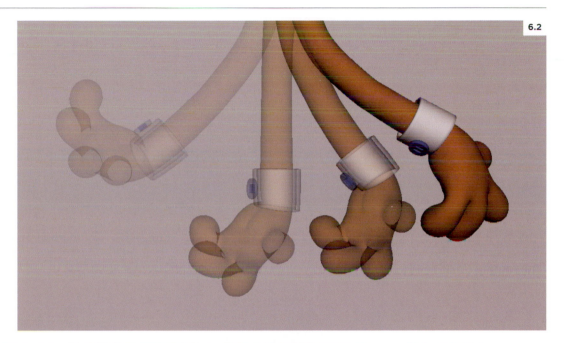

6.2

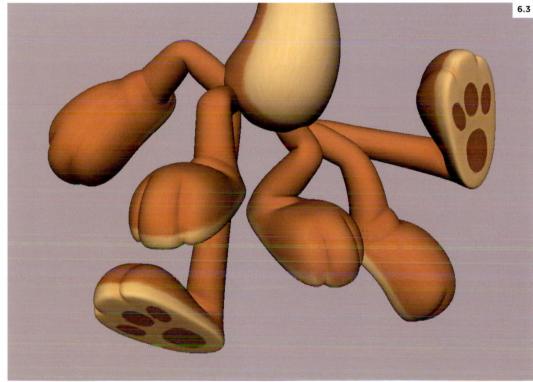

6.3

6.3 Scattered limbs

Here's an example of scattered limbs where there's an element of randomness and chaos. This is particularly useful for a fast running action, where the character is stationary, scrambling their feet to get traction.

Creating Multiples

When creating multiple limbs, the process is entirely dependent on the capability of the rig. If the rig is designed with multiple limbs built in, it's often just a matter of switching on the visibility of the extra limb and posing accordingly. The character rig supplied with this book, Mr. Buttons, is one such rig. He has an additional three arms and three legs for you to use. We'll cover how to do this in detail in the walkthrough at the end of the chapter. But even for rigs that don't have this capability built in, you can still create multiple limbs relatively easily. Here's the process:

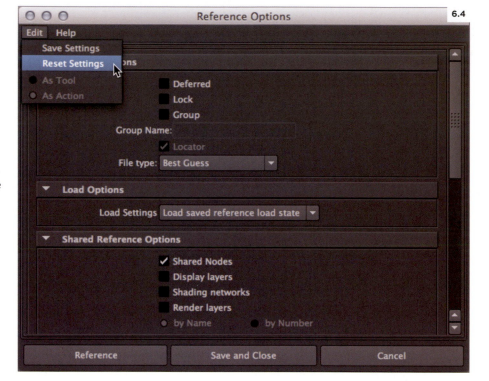

1. Go to the frame where you want to create your multiples.

2. Reference in the same character into your scene so you now have two of the same characters in the scene file. Please make sure you're using the defaults when referencing, as Maya will give each additional character a unique namespace to avoid name-clashing problems.

3. Copy the same exact pose from the original character to the newly referenced character so they are placed right on top of each other. Your rig might have come with a GUI that allows you to select every attribute of each character, making the copying and pasting of the

pose an easy task. If that's not the case, you can fairly quickly do this the old-school way by copying and pasting the controls manually. Select the control(s) you want to copy from, right-click in the timeline, and choose Copy from the pop-up menu. Then select the control(s) on the character you want to paste onto, right-click in the timeline, and choose Paste > Paste from the pop-up menu. You can copy and paste more than one control at a time, but you have to make sure you're selecting them in the same order; otherwise, you'll get unexpected results.

4. Now select the limb you want to be a multiple, and simply change its position to be trailing behind.

6.4 Referencing
When referencing, make sure to use Maya's defaults so that each reference has a unique name.

| THE PROBLEM OF MOTION BLUR | MOTION LINES AND DRY-BRUSH | SMEARS | STAGGERS | INTERVIEW: JASON GIGLIOZZI | STEP-BY-STEP WALKTHROUGH | OVER TO YOU! |

MULTIPLE LIMBS

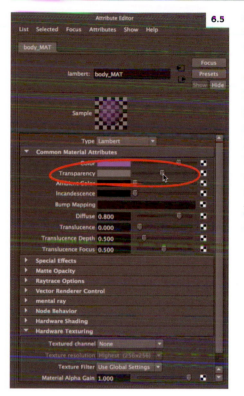

6.5

6.5 Transparency Slider
If you're working with a character other than Mr. Buttons, you can adjust the transparency slider on the shader for that body part to get the right amount of transparency for each additional limb.

5. Getting the multiples to be a different level of transparency is pretty straightforward as well, but it does require adjusting the transparency value of the shader associated with the body part. To do this, right-click on the geometry of the part you want to make more transparent and choose Material Attributes . . . from the pop-up menu. The Attribute Editor should come up, and if the transparency attribute isn't already connected to something else, you'll be able to adjust its slider and make it more or less transparent.

6. The last thing you'll need to do is turn the visibility off for the entire character except for the frame where you have the multiple limb(s). Some rigs have a visibility attribute for the entire character, and in those cases, it's pretty straightforward—just key it on and off. For rigs that don't have this attribute, you can usually go to the topmost node of the character and animate the visibility on and off from there.

7. For each additional multiple, just repeat steps 1 through 6.

If you're going to create a multiple of the entire character, the process is the same with the exception of step 3. Although you might want to copy and paste the entire pose anyway, so you have a starting point for adjusting the pose and position of the character. This shortcut doesn't require as much work as starting from a default pose.

6.6

6.6 A whole character multiple
Here we see the whole character being used as a multiple. This is useful when a character has to travel a great distance over one or two frames.

MOTION LINES AND DRY-BRUSH

As a young kid, I had an obsession with drawing Garfield, the lasagna-loving cat from the comic strip of the same name. Even though he was stationary most of the time (hence his girth), anytime I wanted to indicate movement, I'd use the well-known convention of using motion lines radiating around that part of the character. We see it used similarly in traditional animation where the broad spacing of a fast action can be bridged by motion lines that are drawn to follow the action, giving the illusion of motion blur. Like the other approaches outlined in this chapter, they're usually only visible for a frame or two on screen, but they are a very simple, effective technique. They also tend to be drawn directionally, in the same arc that the character is moving, or are drawn to roughly match the shape of the trailing edge of the character. Occasionally you'll see both styles, giving a slight crosshatched look to the motion lines.

Along the same lines (pun fully intended), dry-brush gives a similar effect. Its name is derived from the technique of using a dry paintbrush, where the paint was applied to the top of the animation cel, giving it a textured look. The brushstroke would usually start out thick and taper as it trailed behind the action. One extreme example of this is when the Looney Tunes Tasmanian Devil would turn into a tornado. To get the high-speed look, the tornado itself was dry-brushed on top of the animation cel. Occasionally we'd see parts of the character escaping the tornado, creating a chaotic and comedic effect.

For 2D folks, achieving this look was as simple as either drawing the lines in with a pencil (motion lines), or painting atop the cel with a sweeping brushstroke (dry-brush). In 3D, we're not so lucky. Now you can also do something similar in post, importing the animation into Photoshop or After Effects and using their set of tools to achieve a similar look, but to keep things all within Maya and have the greatest control, we're going to need to rely on an additional asset that we can reference into our scene. It's called Swoosh, and you can find a link to download it at the companion website.

To use Swoosh, reference it into Maya, and use the controllers to get the desired shape, width, and color. It's important to note that Swoosh is versatile enough to be used for both motion lines and dry-brush. Motion lines will usually be thinner and consistent in color, whereas dry-brush will usually start out thicker and taper the further away it is from the character. With dry-brush, it's also often touching or even covering the part of the character that it's trailing behind. You can adjust the transparency of either end of the asset to create a tapering effect. Check out the walkthrough at the end of the chapter for how I went about using Swoosh within the animated example. Although not as painless as drawing a line, creating motion lines and dry-brush with Swoosh is still a relatively easy way to get this look in Maya.

THE PROBLEM OF
MOTION BLUR

MULTIPLE LIMBS

**MOTION LINES AND
DRY-BRUSH**

SMEARS

STAGGERS

INTERVIEW:
JASON GIGLIOZZI

STEP-BY-STEP
WALKTHROUGH

OVER TO YOU!

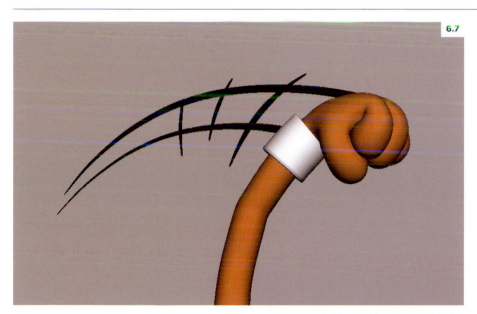

6.7

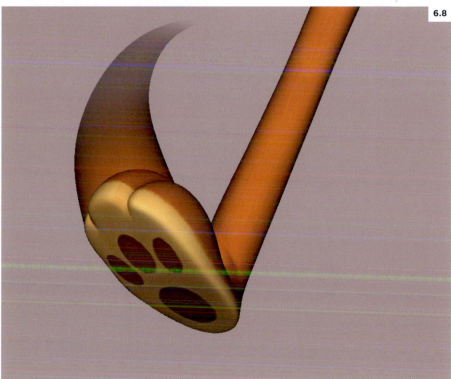

6.8

6.7 Motion lines
Motion lines can either be in the same direction, be parallel to the motion, or be representative of the trailing edge of the character, going in a perpendicular fashion. Here we see both in action.

6.8 Dry-brush effect
The dry-brush look can be achieved by adjusting the scale and transparency of the Swoosh asset. If you're savvy with shader networks, you can also apply a texture to the shader to get a more dry-brush look.

SMEARS

As the name implies, smears are where the character or parts of the character are smeared to cover a large spacing gap. The character is being deformed to such a degree that any semblance of anatomy is thrown out the window. It's completely unrealistic, a total cheat, and a wonderful one at that. Like multiple limbs and motion lines, smears can be used as a substitute for motion blur. Smears are also one of the more amusing techniques to both observe and incorporate into your scene. Advance frame by frame through the Warner Bros. short, *The Dover Boys at Pimento University* (1942), and you'll see prime examples of smears being used liberally throughout the film. *Dover Boys* is also one of the most extreme examples of smears where the smeared frame covers the entire distance when the character moves from point A to point B. You'll notice, too, as with most of these techniques covered here, that it usually resolves in one to two frames. Any longer and it becomes too apparent and could draw attention to itself, taking the audience out of the story.

6.9

Smears like the ones observed in *Dover Boys* are fairly uncommon in CG. From an artistic point of view, going to that extreme with smears isn't always necessary. If a hand is swooping quickly across the screen, dragging and elongating the fingers can be sufficient. Generally speaking, the faster and broader the action, the more you'll want to distort and smear the parts of the character. From a technical point of view, we don't see extreme smears because many rigs aren't designed to be distorted in this manner. Occasionally, you'll find some rigs where parts of the body can be scaled, but the amount of distortion is fairly limited, and you'll start to get some really undesirable deformations in the rig if it's pushed too far. Fortunately for us, Bo Sayre, a Maya scripting guru, has developed the tool, boSmear, to give us this flexibility. We'll discuss that next.

6.9 Scaling
Scaling parts of the character may be adequate when going for the smeared effect, where just a portion of the character is distorted. In this example, Mr. Buttons's nose is squashed to create drag during a quick head turn.

THE PROBLEM OF
MOTION BLUR

MULTIPLE LIMBS

MOTION LINES AND
DRY-BRUSH

SMEARS

STAGGERS

INTERVIEW:
JASON GIGLIOZZI

STEP-BY-STEP
WALKTHROUGH

OVER TO YOU!

boSmear

For individual parts, a flexible, scalable rig can do the trick nicely. But if you want to do some crazy smearing on an entire character, boSmear is the answer. You can find the link to it on the companion website. The way boSmear works is that it creates a polygonal mesh that's placed in front of the lens of a camera that allows you to manipulate the vertices on that mesh, thereby distorting the character that's behind it. When you first launch boSmear, you'll be presented with a GUI with several options (see Figure 6.10). Here's a rundown of each of the options:

6.10 The boSmear tool

Here's a snapshot of the GUI for the boSmear tool, which creates the poly mesh that will be manipulated to create the distortion.

Camera

This is to select the camera that the poly mesh will be attached to. Make sure to select the camera that will be used for the final render and not the perspective camera.

Resolution

These two fields correspond to the number of vertices, both horizontal and vertical, that are created on the poly mesh. The more vertices you have, the more you can fine-tune the smear. However, for most smears, the defaults work just fine.

Target

In this field, you'll want to select a part on the character that the deformations will be centered around. In most cases, the main body control of the character is going to work best. Just select that control and choose Get.

Geometry

Here is where you'll want to add all the parts of the character that you want to be deformed. Just select those parts and click the Add button.

Create Smear

After you've gone through those steps, select Create Smear to create the poly mesh plane that will drive the deformations of the geometry in the list. An Animation Controls menu will pop up to allow you to hide, key, and reset the mesh.

Smear Controls Window

If you happen to close the Animation Controls window, this button will restore it.

At this point, you're ready to start manipulating the mesh in front of the camera. You can do this by right-clicking on the mesh and choosing the type of component you want to use to adjust it. I almost always use vertices with a combination of soft-selection, which can be toggled on and off using the B key. Soft-select provides a nice falloff around the selected vertices, giving pleasing results. By holding down the B key and middle-mouse-button dragging, you can adjust the amount of falloff. Now, you can have at it and start playing around. It's important to note that this doesn't in any way affect the animation you've keyed on your character. This is a separate layer that works independently of the character rig. So you can still tweak and animate your character while it's being deformed by the mesh. When you're ready to start saving what you've created, the following is a list of the options available to you in the Animation Controls window.

6.11 Animation Controls
The GUI for the Animation Controls allows you to key, reset, and hide the poly mesh.

Smear Mesh
You can have more than one smear mesh in your scene. Select the one you want to control.

Toggle Mesh Visibility
Obviously enough, this button turns the visibility of the mesh on and off.

Reset Mesh
This will reset the vertices of the mesh to their default positions.

Key All Mesh Verts
This is how you'll be able to keyframe your smears, so after you've created your smear, click this button, go to the frames before and after the smear, reset the mesh, and then click this button again to make sure the smear only shows on the intended frame.

Show Keys in the Graph Editor
If you need access to the keyframe data on the mesh, this button will make it visible in the Graph Editor.

THE PROBLEM OF
MOTION BLUR

MULTIPLE LIMBS

MOTION LINES AND
DRY-BRUSH

SMEARS

STAGGERS

INTERVIEW:
JASON GIGLIOZZI

STEP-BY-STEP
WALKTHROUGH

OVER TO YOU!

Lastly, there are some additional attributes available to you in the channel box when you have the mesh selected. Here's a rundown of what they do.

6.12

Channel Box / Layer Editor

Channels   Edit   Object   Show

smearMesh

Visibility on
Smear Weight 1
Smear Soften 4
Smear Depth Scale 12
Smear Depth Guide 0

6.12 Channel Box

Occasionally, you may need to tweak these settings for the poly mesh. They can be found in the channel box when the poly mesh is selected.

Smear Weight

This attribute allows you to dial up or down the amount of smearing. The default is set to 1.

Smear Soften

If you notice some tearing geometry on your character, adjusting this attribute may help resolve the issue. The higher the value, the more the smear will be softened. The Default is set to 4.

Smear Depth Scale

If parts of your character are either closer or further away from the camera and are not included in the smear, you can increase the depth of the smear to include them.

Smear Depth Guide

This is a visibility toggle that allows you to see the boundaries of the deformation. It's helpful to have this turned on when adjusting the Smear Depth Scale.

6.13 Smeared

Here we see a smear image of Mr. Buttons, showing the previous and next frame as well. This was created with the help of boSmear.

6.13

151

STAGGERS

Unlike the previous techniques, a stagger has nothing to do with addressing the problem of motion blur. Instead, a stagger is an effect where the character is usually straining and vibrating as they're continuing in a given direction, until they've reached their extreme pose. To achieve this look, we're going to employ a "two frames forward, one frame back" approach and we're going to be using arithmetic to get there. "But I was told there'd be no math!" may be what you're grumbling to yourself—but I promise that the math will be very simple indeed. The setup is a little tricky to get at first, but once you've gone through it a couple of times, you'll be just fine. I'd encourage you to read through the process first so you can get a better grasp on how this is achieved before diving right in. Here's the process:

6.14

6.14 Staggered
Staggers are great for when your character is straining, pushing or pulling on a heavy object. They're also great for vibrating into a Tex Avery style take as seen here.

1. A stagger requires a beginning and ending pose, so make sure you have both of them created before starting. Don't worry about how you're going to interpolate between them at this point. That will be addressed later. Typically, a stagger will be composed of roughly similar poses, with the ending pose being an exaggerated version of the starting pose. Staggering between poses that are strikingly different will often result in a vibrating mess.

2. Determine the duration of the stagger, and make sure you have enough room in your timeline for the number of frames your character will be staggering. A 12 to 16 frame duration seems to be fine for most staggers. So if you're going for a 16-frame stagger, in the timeline, if the beginning pose starts at frame 100, the ending pose will be at frame 116. You'll also want to not put any keyframes in between those two poses, as you'll be overwriting them with new keyframes later.

3. Next, copy and paste those two poses at the end or your animation, where we can have a bit of a workspace, a blank area to work in that's free of any animation. The right-click method of copying and pasting in the timeline will work but you might find the middle-mouse-button dragging method of copying animation to be quicker. The animation in this workspace will become the source animation for our stagger, and we'll copy this animation in a specific order, back to our original location in the timeline. When doing this, though, you'll want to halve the number of frames needed for the stagger. So if your entire animation ends at frame 280, consider copying the beginning pose of the stagger at frame 300 and the ending pose at 308 (16-frame duration, halved). The reason we do this is because staggering works by repeating certain frames over and over again, and our source animation for the stagger only needs to be half the number of frames.

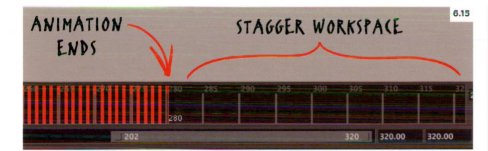

6.15

ANIMATION ENDS

STAGGER WORKSPACE

6.15 Making room

When creating a stagger, not only do you need to make room for it in your animation, but you also need to make room for a workspace area at the very end of your animation so you can copy and paste the stagger poses in the correct sequence.

4. Now that we have our poses in the workspace area at the end of the animation, we need to interpolate between those key poses. You'll almost always want to slow-in to the last pose. For the first pose, however, we can either slow-out or fast-out. Which one to choose? If the action preceding the stagger is fast, like a Tex Avery-style take, a fast-out approach makes the most sense. If your character is straining, while pushing against a giant boulder, for instance, since the action is more gradual, you might want to slow-out from the first pose. I find that using the linear (fast-out) and flat (slow-out) tangent types usually do the trick nicely without having to pull on any tangent handles.

5. Now for the fun part. With the interpolation done, we can now copy frames from the workspace at the end of our animation (frames 300–308) to the original location (frames 100–116). The order in which we do this is crucial, and this is where the math comes in. Remember, we're using a two-frames forward, one-frame back approach so keep that in mind while you're copying and

pasting your frames. You don't need to copy from frame 300 since that's identical to the pose on frame 100. So go forward two frames to 302, copy and paste that to the next frame at the original location, frame 101. Now, returning to the workspace, go back one frame, to 301, copy and paste that to the next frame at the original location, frame 102. Now, go forward two frames to 303, copy and paste that to the next frame at the original location, frame 103. Now, go back one frame, to 302, copy and paste that to the next frame at the original location, frame 104. Continue this two-frames forward, one-frame back process until you're done. Now the math doesn't work out exactly so you should end up one frame shy when you've pasted the last frame. You can then delete that last frame on 116 and frame 115 will become the last frame of the stagger.

If you're having some difficulty remembering whether you've gone forward or back the last time you copied, you can create a chart in advance to help you with this. This way, if you get lost or confused, you can refer back to this and find your way. Figure 6.16 shows the chart for this example. You'll notice that while we're copying our animation in the two-frames forward, one-frame back method, we're actually pasting sequentially, in one-frame increments. This is what creates the staggering effect. Once you're done and are happy with the results, you can delete the animation in your workspace.

6.16

WORKSPACE (copy)	ANIMATION (paste)
300	100
302	101
301	102
303	103
302	104
304	105
303	106
305	107
304	108
306	109
305	110
307	111
306	112
308	113
307	114
308	115

6.16 Stagger chart

Here's an example of a stagger chart, which can be extremely useful if you forget your place when going through this process.

TIP | USING RESTRAINT

There's a tendency when incorporating techniques like these to make them the centerpiece of the animation. As animation nerds, we love to seek out and geek out over these wonderfully crazy frames. So much so that when students first try their hand at creating them, the tendency is to have a little pancake with our syrup, instead of the other way around. These effects are not meant to become the main thing, so we don't want to just create animation as a showpiece for our cartoony animation chops. While you're learning this stuff, by all means, dive in and go nuts. But when you're creating animation for an audience other than yourself, practice the art of restraint and only use these techniques for those special moments that call for it.

JASON FIGLIOZZI

I had the good fortune of knowing Jason Figliozzi when he was a student at Ringling College of Art and Design. It was there that he created the delightfully cartoony short film, *Snack Attack* (2008). He's since gone on to have a wonderful career as an animator, working on *Cloudy with a Chance of Meatballs* (2009), *Tangled* (2010), and, most recently, *Big Hero 6* (2014). He took some time out of his busy schedule to answer a handful of questions.

What inspired you to pursue animation as a career?

I always wanted to be a cartoonist. I took these classes outside of school, probably when I was about seven until I was 18. I then worked for a guy teaching art and cartooning. His name was Rich, and he'd go to the Saratoga racetrack in upstate New York, and he would sell cartoons about horseracing. Then he got into more realistic, stylized oil painting, and he still does it today. He made a living off of that, so I think that was the first time that I thought you could make a living off of artwork. But I think the pivotal point of wanting to do computer animation was in high school. I was in 11th grade, and I was taking these Advanced Placement art courses in New York. During that time, I was looking at universities that studied everything, like liberal arts colleges, but they didn't have a concentration in art. Anyway, my teacher handed me the Ringling College catalogue, and I remember seeing all the student artwork in the book, like Patrick Osborne's artwork and a bunch of other people that I have now become friends with. But, seeing that, and looking online at their student short films, I thought that was the coolest thing ever, that you could create something like that. And I realized, I love cartoons, and animated movies especially.

I loved *Toy Story* (1995) when I was a kid and that blew my mind because it was different from any other animated feature. But I really didn't know if I would like it. I did little flipbooks when I was growing up, all throughout high school and stuff, and that was kind of the extent. I didn't know anything about the principles of animation or anything like that until I went to Ringling.

So now that you are doing it for a living, do you still like it?

Oh yeah! I mean, there are those times when it gets pretty crazy, with long hours, struggling to stay healthy, not seeing your loved ones very much and stuff like that. But when you see your work on the big screen and you see people, the way they react to it, it's really very cool. It's one thing to have other artists react to what you're doing, which is great, but when you see a whole theater full of people reacting to what you did, it makes it all worthwhile.

So let's go back to your Ringling days. You created this short film *Snack Attack*, which had a really, very cartoony style, not just for a student film, but also it was really kind of pushing the boundaries of what was being done in computer animation at that time. What caused you to go in that direction with your short film?

It started before senior year, in preproduction for our short film, but I wanted to try and see what I could do. I was a fan of Warner Bros.'s cartoons growing up, but it was during that time that I saw the *Dover Boys* short film for the first time. I had never seen anything like it before, and I thought that it would be amazing to create something so stylized, pushing the animation to that point. I think a lot of parts in that short are way too overdone, looking back on it.

But that's kind of the fun in it, you push the hell out of it, and try to see what you can do, and pull back from there. I'm still guilty of doing that in all my shots. I usually go overboard, and then I have to reel it back in to reality. That squashing, stretching stuff can be really funny, and I think what I really wanted to do with that short was make people laugh. And just trying to do something different, I think.

Like *Dover Boys*, you created these crazy smear frames. Now at the time, there were no easy tools for helping with that, so what was the process for creating those?
Some things were kind of just trial and error, kind of seeing what worked, but I had separate rigs for some shots, trying to figure out what was needed. Much of It was built into the rig, but it became really, really slow. I used lattice deformers for some stuff, and I also scaled parts of the character, seeing how

far I could push it. Jamil Lahham, another Ringling student—he and I were talking about it because he had a different approach to it. I think his was to just throw a lattice deformer on it, using it for that specific frame, wherever you wanted to control the shape. For some reason, maybe some OCD thing I have, I had to have it in the rig. It was really just Frankensteined together, and it wasn't anything amazing. It wasn't exactly what I wanted—nothing ever turns out the way you really want it to, but you get it to a certain point, and that's when you call it quits. I think some of it was pretty successful.

It's such a departure from what you normally see from student films that it got the attention of Sony, who hired you to work on *Cloudy with a Chance of Meatballs*. Do you feel like your experience on *Snack Attack* helped you transition smoothly into that?
I think it did. Pete Nash, who was the head of animation there at the time, who hired me, I think that's what grabbed his attention. But I remember they were worried about acting, because I didn't really have that much good acting on my student reel. I really learned that side of things at Sony, stuff I never really dove into at Ringling. But I got to work on some really fun shots on *Cloudy*.

**The main thing is don't be afraid to try something different. I think it's important to stay away from the cliché. So if you think of something weird and different, you might as well try it out and see what people think of it...
JASON FIGLIOZZI**

After *Cloudy*, you left Sony to work on *Tangled* at Disney. *Tangled* seemed to be like a huge step forward for Disney animation, especially computer animation. Do you feel like that was a natural progression of the art, or was there something different going on at Disney that caused them to kind of leapfrog in terms of quality?

I think it has a lot to do with the leadership on that show, John Kahrs and Clay Kaytis. And of course, Glen Keane, who was working on it as well. Clay and John were the heads of animation, but Glen was kind of like another head of animation. Glen's 2D sensibilities are crazy amazing. He was pushing the boundaries and people were like, I don't think we can do that with CG. And he was like, you have to be able to push it, and he would sketch things and say I think we can do that. We would try to live up to that and take the essence of what he was drawing. One thing I loved in that movie was the posing. The posing, just frame by frame, is pretty incredible. The acting choices were great, and the rigs were great for the time. It was like a new step forward in the rigging.

Really, I think it came down to who was pushing us to try different things and push the acting choices. Kahrs is amazing at just looking at

a shot once and pointing out that it needs this little spark, you know, and it will add that much more to the shot. Things you've never thought of. Having that eye on your shot, and Clay is the same exact way. They've both been in the industry a long time. And Glen, being there to push the poses and push pretty much everything. That was just something that I had never really experienced and a lot of people there didn't experience it either. It's kind of hard to explain. And we've been trying to improve upon it ever since.

It was kind of cool in that, from my perspective, it seemed like a lot of schools were chasing after the Pixar style. And I think that some of the studios were doing the same thing. *Tangled* seemed to skew away from that and was something kind of new and different in computer animation.

I think it really comes from the hand-drawn background of the studio. Even when you look at old Disney movies, the acting was great, and the posing was amazing. I think a lot of it comes from knowing where the studio came from and what it's founded upon. Not to say that all the studios don't have that, but Disney has such a rich legacy. I think it helps their movies stand out from the crowd. Animators are better able

to spot the differences, but even a friend of mine was saying that something was different about the animation in *Tangled*—and he's not an animator. Even his parents were saying there was something different about it, but they couldn't put their finger on it. It felt different, you know? And that's pretty cool.

Can you briefly describe your animation process?

It depends on what the shot is and what is being asked of me. I always start with video reference. Video reference is definitely one of those things where you can avoid pulling from the same bag of tricks. Everyone has those tricks they do over and over again, and shooting video reference can help you get out of that, and find something new to put in your shot. From there I take a look at the reference, and if it's a physical shot, I'll study it to make sure I know exactly what my body is doing in the reference because I find physical mechanics very difficult. From there I'll block, probably on fours and sixes, to get the general timing of the entire shot from start to finish. Even though it's my first pass, I'll try to make the best pose I can. For some reason, I cannot move on to the next thing until I get the pose to where I like it. I can't just do

6.17

something sloppy and then move on to save time.

I'll then work on my timing and break it down from there. If there's a certain part of the animation that I really want to sell to the director, I will break that down as much as I can before showing it. For me, the purpose of showing it the first time is to sell your idea. If it doesn't come across clearly, an idea will be given to you, and then it won't be yours anymore. You don't want to have a shot that's someone else's idea. It's no longer yours, and you don't feel the same about it anymore. You don't have the passion for it anymore so I think it's very important to do whatever you can to sell your shot. Then I show that to the directors, and if I get a buy-off, I'll pretty much bring it to the end and show it again for any last-minute polish moments.

What advice do you have for students entering the field?

The main thing is don't be afraid to try something different. I think it's important to stay away from the cliché. So if you think of something weird and different, you might as well try it out and see what people think of it. It's worth trying something out of the box and getting denied rather than not trying it at all. Also, get as many eyes on your work as you can— the more eyes, the better. Because in the end, you're not going to be the only one looking at your work. It's not about your reaction to it, it's about everyone else's. Getting as many people to look at your work as possible is only going to make it better.

6.17 *Snack Attack*, **2008**
Here are frames from some of the more cartoony moments from Jason Figliozzi's short film. As you can see, Jason made ingenious use of smears in lieu of motion blur.

STEP-BY-STEP WALKTHROUGH   Adding Multiples

In this walkthrough, I'll be going through the application of each of the different techniques discussed in the chapter to put the finishing touches to our animation.

1. When Mr. Buttons is desperately wanting to escape, he's running in place, midair, trying to get some traction (See Figure 6.18). Because his feet are moving so fast, it's the perfect opportunity to introduce multiple legs. For this action, I was initially going to go with random legs placement, showing chaotic action. But after I keyed in the running action of his feet, there was a circular pattern going on, so I thought it'd be best to use the multiples to reinforce that and bridge some of the large spacing gaps caused by his four-frame run cycle. A typical run cycle can be anywhere from six to eight frames, so we're working with roughly half of that.

2. If you're working with Mr. Buttons, multiple arms and legs are built into the rig. You can access them from the main body control, and you'll see the channels for the extra arms and legs. The attributes go from 0 to 1, with 0 being hidden to 1 being fully visible. You can adjust the transparency of the limbs by dialing in a number anywhere in between (see Figure 6.19). Mr. Buttons can have up to three additional multiples of each limb.

6.18

6.19

Channel Box / Layer Editor	
Channels Edit Object Show	
Mr_Buttons:Mr_Buttons_COG_Ctrl	
Translate X	1.617
Translate Y	3.084
Translate Z	23.409
Rotate X	167.29
Rotate Y	-35.539
Rotate Z	-160.984
Multiples	
L Arm 1	0
L Arm 2	0
L Arm 3	0
R Arm 1	0
R Arm 2	0
R Arm 3	0
L Leg 1	0.22
L Leg 2	0
L Leg 3	0
R Leg 1	0.7
R Leg 2	0.2
R Leg 3	0

THE PROBLEM OF
MOTION BLUR

MULTIPLE LIMBS

MOTION LINES AND
DRY-BRUSH

SMEARS

STAGGERS

INTERVIEW:
JASON GIGLIOZZI

STEP-BY-STEP
WALKTHROUGH

OVER TO YOU!

3. Start by adding one limb in at a time. Figure 6.20 shows the first one I've added in. I've posed it, following the action of the main leg. It's helpful to go back to the previous frame to see where the leg was before to get an idea of direction and speed. Keep in mind that you still need to pay attention to the spacing and arcs. So if you want to get a circular action going on, you'll need to arc it appropriately. After I'd posed it, I adjusted the transparency slightly to make it less opaque.

4. Working sequentially, I added in another multiple leg (see Figure 6.21). On this one, the spacing is greater, and it is a little more transparent, creating a fade-off look, the further away we get from the main leg. I can have up to three of each limb, but I've decided that just one more will do the trick nicely. The spacing gap has been addressed, and adding more could muddy it up. One thing to be mindful of is that the transparency setting should be adjusted according to the final output. If it's rendered, the transparency will likely be different than if it's playblasted.

5. For the other leg, I added just one multiple (see Figure 6.22). Why not keep it consistent and match the number of multiples on the other leg? I did this for a couple of reasons. For starters, just like I stopped at two multiples on the other leg, I don't want to muddy things up by adding in too many multiples and make it a jumbled mess. And second, the distance traveled for this leg is less than the other one. Again, I can reference the previous frame for how best to judge this. All that being said, the true test will be to see it in action. I've got about a dozen more frames to add multiples to and it won't be until I see them all working together that I get a sense of whether or not I've added in too many or too few or if the transparency is not enough, and so on. Some trial and error is to be expected while you're working this stuff out.

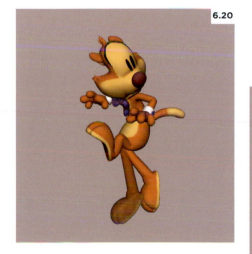

6.20

6.21

6.22

Motion Lines and Dry-Brush Effect

1. At the very end of the animation, Mr. Buttons quickly leaves the frame, and when played back in real time it almost looks as if he's disappeared. We have some indication of his movement with the few frames that precede his vanishing act (as seen in Figure 6.23), but because it happens so fast, we need to add some motion lines to further indicate his screen-left departure. And just to clarify, the images in Figure 6.23 are in reverse order so you can better see the flow of his movement. As with multiple limbs, it's important that we refer back to the previous frames. When adding in the motion lines, they should match the path of action and looking at the previous frames will reveal that.

2. For these motion lines, I'll be using the Swoosh asset that you can download from the companion website. Be sure to reference these into your scene. For each additional motion line, you'll need to reference in a new asset. You'll find instructions on how to use it along with the asset on the website. I started adding motion lines on the frame right before he leaves the screen because the spacing is a little broad between this frame and the frame before it (see Figure 6.24). Just to reiterate, while adding in motion lines, I'm constantly page-flipping between this frame and the frame before it, so I can properly map out the curve of the motion lines, looking at the path of action of each of the parts.

3. I've added in a few more motion lines and I also changed their color to more closely match Mr. Buttons (Figure 6.25). By default, Swoosh comes in black, which is drawing too much attention to itself, so I went for something more subtle. Since there's no texture on the Swoosh, you can easily change the color by adjusting the shader that's applied to the asset.

6.23

6.24

6.25

4. Now that I have finished that frame, I'm moving on to the next frame, placing more motion lines. Just as you did with the multiple limbs, you'll need to keyframe the visibility on and off, so the motion lines only appear in the frame on which you want them to be seen (see Figure 6.26). You can change the visibility of the entire Swoosh asset by going to the top node of the hierarchy and keying the visibility on and off there. However, since Mr. Buttons has left the building, so to speak, I've kept the motion lines visible from the previous frame to help me determine the placement and curvature of the new ones.

5. Since Mr. Buttons is covering such a great distance here, I also wanted to add a dry-brush effect to reduce some of the empty space. Believe it or not, the giant orange log shown in Figure 6.27 is going to be the dry-brush effect. I've scaled up the Swoosh asset to cover up most of the motion lines and made the color orange, again to more closely match Mr. Buttons. However, this looks really odd, so we need to add some transparency to it to taper it off.

6. With the Swoosh asset, each of the controls used to determine the shape of the geometry have a Transparency attribute you can adjust. In Figure 6.28, I simply dialed it all the way up on the tail-end of the Swoosh to create a nice falloff. Again, when dealing with transparency, what you see in a playblast will likely be different than a rendered image, so if your final output is going to be lit and rendered, be sure to do some testing first.

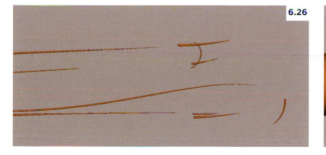

6.26

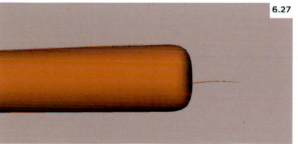

6.27

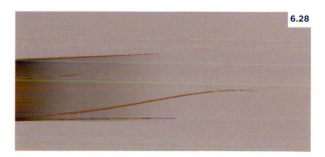

6.28

Smears

1. So far in this walkthrough we've covered how to implement multiple limbs and motion lines/dry-brush. Let's now turn our attention to smears (see Figure 6.29). The plan is to take this existing pose, which you may recall seeing in Chapter 4, and use the boSmear tool to deform the entire character. In looking at the GUI, I selected the main camera that we've set up to render (not the perspective view), to be the view the smear will be constrained to. I selected the body control to be the Target and then added all the character geometry to be a part of the deformation. After this, I clicked on Create Smear, and now I'm ready to start smearing Mr. Buttons.

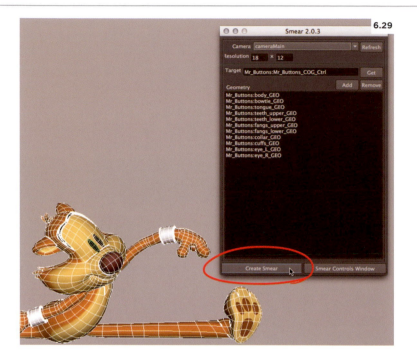

2. After you've created the smear, you should see what appears to be a faint ghosted plane appear in front of the camera, as in Figure 6.30. This is the mesh you can manipulate to drive the deformation on the character. Also, for some reason, if you have the smooth-mesh preview turned on, your character will return to lo-res poly view. Just select the character and press the 3 key, and you'll be returned to the smoothed-mesh mode. Right-click the newly created mesh in front of the lens and choose Vertex. Now we can manipulate the mesh on the component level and, in so doing, smear Mr. Buttons.

THE PROBLEM OF
MOTION BLUR

MULTIPLE LIMBS

MOTION LINES AND
DRY-BRUSH

SMEARS

STAGGERS

INTERVIEW:
JASON GIGLIOZZI

STEP-BY-STEP
WALKTHROUGH

OVER TO YOU!

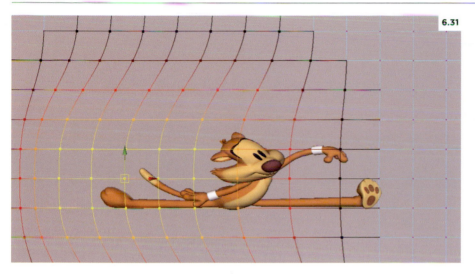

6.31

4. Don't be shy about pulling the vertices around. In fact, the mesh may get pretty messy, with vertices overlapping. Just as we're not concerned with pretty curves in the Graph Editor, we're not concerned with a pretty mesh in front of the lens. All that matters is what the character looks like. That being said, if your mesh gets too out of control, you can always reset it by using the Reset Mesh button in the Smear Controls Window, which is accessible from the boSmear window (see Figure 6.32).

3. You can move the vertices around individually, but I'd recommend starting by moving groups of them (see Figure 6.31). I'd also strongly recommend you use soft-select to get a nice falloff around your selected vertices. You can turn soft-select on and off by using the B hotkey. Holding down the B key while left-mouse-button dragging right and left will increase and decrease the amount of falloff, respectively. I've noticed that sometimes when I first turn on soft-select, the falloff radius is huge, and all the vertices are highlighted yellow. In that case, just continue to reduce the size of the falloff until it becomes a more manageable size.

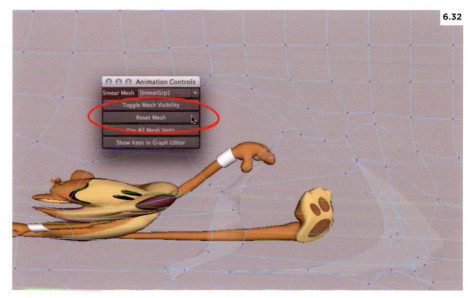

6.32

5. Since the smear mesh is just a polygonal plane, you can use any number of Maya's tools to manipulate the mesh. The Sculpt Geometry Tool is particularly useful (see Figure 6.33). First, make sure that you're in the Polygons module, then go to Mesh > Sculpt Geometry Tool > Option Box. This will allow the tool settings to pop up for this tool, and you can choose different brushes for manipulating the smear mesh. My favorite is the Relax tool, circled here. This allows you to bring the mesh back to a more relaxed, default state, useful if you have vertices that have gone astray. Simply select the mesh (not the vertices), and paint away. And just as with soft-select, you can hold down the B hotkey to make the brush larger and smaller by dragging the left mouse button right and left.

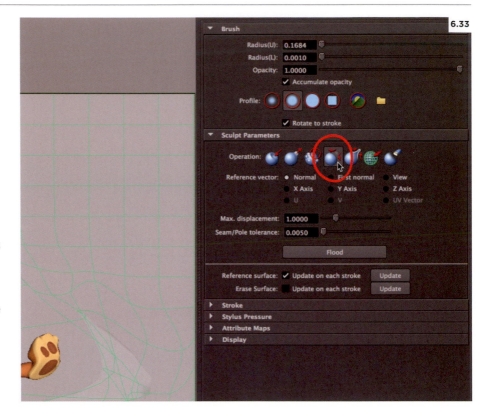

6. One thing you may have noticed is that if you frame forward and backward, the deformation applies to every frame. To fix this, first open the Smear Controls window by clicking on the lower right button of the same name in the original boSmear window. Now click on the Key All Mesh Verts on the frame where you want to apply the smear (see Figure 6.34). Then go to the previous frame, and click on the Reset Mesh button to remove the deformation followed by Key All Mesh Verts. Do the same for the frame right after the smear. You can then click on Toggle Mesh Visibility to hide the mesh. And now you're done!

Staggers

1. One last, but certainly not least, cartoony technique is the stagger. Staggers are actually my favorite technique of the bunch. This is partially true because they're one of the easier techniques to implement but also because they look really cool when done right. Shown in Figure 6.35 is the sequence of poses that culminate in a stagger into the last pose.

2. As already mentioned, we need a starting and ending pose. I'm tempted to use the pose where he's folded over like a taco, the second-to-last pose in the sequence, but staggering from that pose into the final one would be too big of a change and vibrate too violently. So I need to create a pose that's close to the final pose but a little less extreme. I simply copied the ending pose and dialed it back some. Figure 6.36 shows the beginning and end poses for the stagger I'll be creating.

6.35

6.36

3. My stagger will begin on frame 240 and end on frame 252. I've decided to go with a 12-frame stagger, since I don't want Mr. Buttons to have too much hang-time before tearing out of there. I'll be using some space at the end of the animation as a workspace to copy from. The last frame of my animation is 276 so I copied the start and end poses to frames 300 and 306, as shown in Figure 6.37. Why did I halve the time to six frames instead of 12? Again, staggering works by repeating certain frames so I only need in my workspace half the number of what's needed for the actual animation.

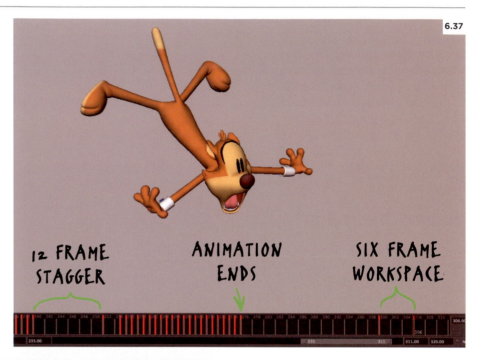

6.37

12 FRAME STAGGER

ANIMATION ENDS

SIX FRAME WORKSPACE

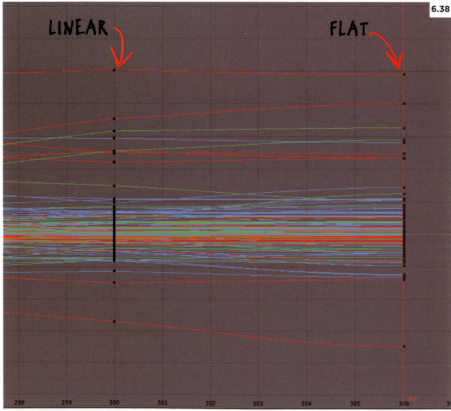

6.38

LINEAR

FLAT

4. Using the Graph Editor, I framed the curves so I could see the two poses that I just copied to the workspace. In order to get the stagger to have a fast-out, slow-in feel, I changed the tangents of the first pose to linear and the tangents on the last pose to flat (see Figure 6.38).

THE PROBLEM OF
MOTION BLUR

MULTIPLE LIMBS

MOTION LINES AND
DRY-BRUSH

SMEARS

STAGGERS

INTERVIEW:
JASON GIGLIOZZI

STEP-BY-STEP
WALKTHROUGH

OVER TO YOU!

5. Lastly, I copied and pasted from the workspace to the animation, using the two frames forward, one frame back approach. As I mentioned earlier in the chapter, it can be helpful to chart this out in case you get lost somewhere in the process. Figure 6.39 shows my chart for this stagger. When you're finished with the copying and pasting, playblast the animation and see how it looks. If it doesn't look quite right, it's not too difficult to make changes. If the stagger is too broad, you can edit the starting pose to more closely match the final pose. Perhaps it's a timing issue and you'd like to add more or less frames to the stagger. Those changes are fairly easy to implement, so feel free to experiment to achieve different results. When you're happy, just delete the two keyframes in the workspace, and you're done!

6.39

WORKSPACE (copy)	ANIMATION (paste)
300	240
302	241
301	242
303	243
302	244
304	245
303	246
305	247
304	248
306	249
305	250
306	251

You've saved the best part for last, and now it's time to jump in and start playing around with these cartoony techniques.

Give yourself plenty of time and plenty of forgiveness, as you're bound to make some mistakes along the way. If you're having some difficulty with one technique, try another one out to see if you'll have better success with it. You can always return later, with a fresher pair of eyes and be better equipped to tackle it.

Keep at it, and in the end you'll have created something frame-by-frame worthy.

CONCLUSION

When I was given the opportunity to teach animation for the first time, I immediately panicked because I thought that I was completely out of my depth. I was still learning this stuff myself, so I felt woefully unqualified. And to be perfectly honest, I was. But I took the challenge anyway. As with most things, experience is the best teacher, and I eventually found my footing. I just hope the students I had for those first few years didn't suffer too harshly at the hand of my inexperience. The same held true for when I first dipped my toe in the waters of cartoony animation. This was the stuff I grew up with every afternoon, watching the Looney Tunes shorts, delighting in their crazy antics, so I felt I like knew it well enough. But it's one thing to be an observer and another thing entirely to be in the trenches, doing the actual work. But it's there, in that place of discomfort and uncertainty, where the real learning takes place. Sure, I floundered about in the early stages of exploring this new style of animation, but each failure was an opportunity for growth, and I just kept at it until it began to click.

You may be finding yourself in the same boat. Perhaps you're reading this after you've gone through the book and tried your hand at cartoony animation and have had more failures than successes at this point. If that's you, don't give up. You can do this. It may take a dozen or more attempts, but if you persist, you'll eventually get it right. It might be helpful to take a piecemeal approach to learning cartoony animation. If the pose test is where you struggle the most, just keep creating poses over and over again all the while getting eyes on your work. Experienced or not, outside input is almost always helpful. The same goes for creating breakdowns, refining the motion or some of the crazy techniques outlined in Chapter 6. Whatever weakness you need to shore up, spend your time there so you can continue to develop your skills.

Adding to your skillset is going to make you more marketable. In practical terms, having a breadth of style in your animation reel is one way to get noticed by a studio. My hope is that this book has helped serve that purpose by providing you with the "how-to" to expand your skillset so your work will stand out. But more importantly, I believe for any artist to thrive, there is the need to continue to learn and grow. My greater hope is that this book has inspired you to try a new and different approach to animation—one that will challenge and push you out of your comfort zone and lead you to a richer and more rewarding career as an animation artist. I wish you all the best in this journey.

FURTHER READING

Aside from *The Illusion of Life: Disney Animation* by Ollie Johnston and Frank Thomas and *The Animator's Survival Kit* by Richard Williams—which should be on every animator's bookshelf—here are some books that will help you build your cartoony animation muscles even further:

Character Animation Crash Course
—Eric Goldberg
Eric is a master traditional animator who has distilled years of wisdom in a fun to read and delightfully illustrated book.

Draw the Looney Tunes
—Dan Romanelli
Don't confuse this book with the simplistic how-to drawing books geared for children. This book is full of useful information on drawing in general, and the illustrations are some of the most expressive and beautifully drawn poses I've come across.

Drawn to Life: 20 Golden Years of Disney Master Classes: Volumes 1 & 2
—Walt Stanchfield
These books are perfect for someone looking to better their gesture and thumbnail drawings. We used to pass photocopies of Walt Stanchfield's notes around back in my college days. We cherished each one we could get our hands on. Now they're lovingly published in two volumes of absolute goodness.

Pose Drawing Sparkbook
—Cedric Hohnstadt
This sketchbook contains hundreds of different exercises, designed to jump-start your creative juices and help you develop great storytelling poses.

FURTHER VIEWING

Physical media is on the way out, but there's nothing like a frame-by-frame study of classic animation that DVDs and Blu-rays can provide—something you can't easily do with streaming media. I strongly encourage you to build up your library of Blu-Ray and DVD collections of animated cartoons while you still can. Here are a few I'd highly recommend:

Looney Tunes Golden Collection, Volumes 1–6—DVD and/or
Looney Tunes Platinum Collection, Volumes 1–3—Blu-ray
Each volume contains dozens of beautifully restored Looney Tunes short films.

Walt Disney Treasures DVDs
Want to own just about every Disney animated short film? These DVD sets are out of print and you'll pay a pretty penny for some of them, but they're absolutely worth it.

Tom & Jerry: Golden Collection, Vol. 1—Blu-ray
These classic Tom and Jerry shorts are full of wonderful examples of cartoony action.

Who Framed Roger Rabbit: 25th Anniversary Edition
Who Framed Roger Rabbit is a great animated film in its own right, but the three Roger Rabbit short films, *Tummy Trouble*, *Rollercoaster Rabbit*, and *Trail Mix-Up*, included in this set, are some of the greatest examples of cartoony animation.

INDEX

INDEX

PICTURE CREDITS

1.1 *Star Wars: The Clone Wars* (2008). Lucasfilm / The Kobal Collection

1.2 *The Avengers* (2012). Marvel Enterprises / The Kobal Collection

1.3 *The Flintstones* (1960–1966). Hanna Barbera / The Kobal Collection

1.4 *Cloudy with a Chance of Meatballs* (2009). Sony Pictures Animation / The Kobal Collection

1.5 *Horton Hears a Who!* (2008). Blue Sky / 20th Century Fox / The Kobal Collection

1.6 *Despicable Me* (2010). Universal / The Kobal Collection

1.8 *Star Trek* (2009). Paramount / Bad Robot / The Kobal Collection

1.9 *Cats Don't Dance* (1997). David Kirschner Prod. / The Kobal Collection

1.10 *Shark Tale* (2004). DreamWorks / The Kobal Collection

2.1 *Horton Hears a Who!* (2008). Blue Sky / 20th Century Fox / The Kobal Collection

2.3 Courtesy of Ricardo Jost Resende

2.4 Courtesy of Ricardo Jost Resende

2.5 *Charlie Chaplin* (c. 1920). The Kobal Collection

2.6 *Marlon Brando* (1951). Warner Bros. / The Kobal Collection

2.7 *Pirates of the Caribbean: Dead Man's Chest* (2006). Disney Enterprises Inc. / The Kobal Collection / Mountain, Peter

2.18 Courtesy of Ricardo Jost Resende

3.9 *Rio* (2011). Twentieth Century Fox / The Kobal Collection

3.10 *Despicable Me* (2010). Universal / The Kobal Collection

3.11 *Madagascar 3: Europe's Most Wanted* (2012). DreamWorks Animation / The Kobal Collection

3.12 *Despicable Me* (2010). Universal / The Kobal Collection

3.13 *David* by Buonarroti, Michelangelo, 1501–1504, 16th Century, Full Relief Marble. The Art Archive / Mondadori Portfolio / Electa

3.14 *Horton Hears a Who!* (2008). Blue Sky / 20th Century Fox / The Kobal Collection

3.15 *Kung Fu Panda* (2008). DreamWorks / The Kobal Collection

3.16 *Hotel Transylvania* (2012). Sony Pictures Animation / The Kobal Collection

3.18 *Hotel Transylvania* (2012). Sony Pictures Animation / The Kobal Collection

3.19 *Cloudy with a Chance of Meatballs 2* (2013). Columbia Pictures / Sony Pictures Animation / Spi / The Kobal Collection

3.20 *Cloudy with a Chance of Meatballs* (2009). Sony Pictures Animation / The Kobal Collection

3.21 *Hotel Transylvania* (2012). Sony Pictures Animation / The Kobal Collection

4.1 *Ice Age: The Meltdown* (2006). 20th Century Fox / The Kobal Collection

4.4 *The Vitruvian Man*, also called *The Universal Man, Canon of Proportions* and *Proportions of Man,* Drawing, Late 15th Century, Facsimile, From Original at Gallerie Dell' Accademia, Venice, Italy. Leonardo Da Vinci, 1452–1519. The Art Archive / Private Collection Italy / Gianni Dagli Orti

4.5 *Despicable Me* (2010). Universal / The Kobal Collection

4.6 *Rio* (2011). 20th Century Fox / The Kobal Collection

4.8 *Hotel Transylvania* (2012). Sony Pictures Animation / The Kobal Collection

5.2 *Kung Fu Panda 2* (2011). DreamWorks Animation / The Kobal Collection

5.9 *Horton Hears a Who!* (2008). Blue Sky / 20th Century Fox / The Kobal Collection

5.10 *Monster House* (2006). Columbia / The Kobal Collection

6.1 *Madagascar* (2005). DreamWorks Pictures / The Kobal Collection

6.17 *Snack Attack* (2008). Courtesy of Jason Figliozzi

ACKNOWLEDGMENTS

This book wouldn't have come together without the help of so many wonderful people. Thanks to Georgia Kennedy, my editor, who has guided me through this whole process, offering encouragement, her expertise, and enduring patience with a first-time author.

I would like to extend a special thanks to the interviewees, Ken Duncan, Jason Figliozzi, Ricardo Jost Resende, T. Dan Hofstedt, Pepe Sánchez, and Matt Williames. Their shared wisdom has added immensely to this book.

To my many students who have challenged me and taught me far more than I could ever teach them, thank you. I name every one of my gray hairs after you.

Mr. Buttons and I would like to thank Jeremiah Alcorn, Marcus Ng, and Gabby Zapata. He wouldn't exist without their wonderful contributions.

Thanks to Cheryl Cabrera, who has been my second pair of eyes, working to make this book as helpful as possible to students of animation.

I can't thank my family enough for their continued support. Specifically, I'd like to thank my wife, Debbie. She's my lifelong best friend and soul mate who served as my own personal editor and biggest cheerleader. Thanks go to my oldest daughter, Sarah, who transcribed all the interviews and whose wit and intelligence always keeps me on my toes, and to my youngest daughter, Savannah, whose goofiness and love of life continually inspire me.

Lastly, I'd like to thank God. He has given me the ability and good fortune to make cartoons for a living.

The publishers would like to thank Cheryl Cabrera, Paul Grant, Hugo Glover, Jason Theaker, Eric Patterson, Pete Hriso, and Jesse O'Brien.